Things
Get
Better

Katie Piper

Things Get Better

Quercus

First published in Great Britain in 2012 by
Quercus
55 Baker Street
7th Floor, South Block
London
W1U 8EW

A CIP catalogue record for this book is available
from the British Library.

ISBN 978 1 78087 477 7

10 9 8 7 6 5 4 3 2

Consultant: Christine Webber

Text designed and typeset by Bob Vickers.

Printed and bound in Great Britain by Clays Ltd. St Ives plc.

Contents

Foreword

All I used to know about Katie Piper was that she was a young, beautiful model and TV presenter whose life was utterly devastated when a man threw acid into her face. What I know now – having been lucky enough to meet and work with her – is that there are no superlatives great enough to describe this unique, brave and marvellous woman, who has such a huge capacity to care for others.

The brutal attack, instigated by her ex-boyfriend, literally marked her permanently and changed her life for ever. But because Katie is robustly sane, funny and resilient, she has seized upon what could have been a tragedy and turned it into an incredible triumph. And she has made her future, which is now so different from how she once planned it, fulfilling and exciting, and a marvellous inspiration to all.

Most people, on hearing what happened to Katie, say: 'I'd sooner die than live through all that pain and terror and disfigurement.' And Katie herself admits that before her accident she'd have shared that view. But how lucky we are that she discovered in herself an overwhelming desire to live and to recover – because what she has learned, a very, very hard way, is something that she is bent on sharing with the rest of us.

Through telling her story and setting up her foundation, Katie has already helped countless people. And this book will help thousands more. Katie would be the first to say that she has had excellent treatment for her mind, as well as her body. But as a therapist I know that very few individuals are as keen to participate in learning about themselves in the positive way that she has. And I also know that she has wisdom beyond her years.

Furthermore, Katie has a fine perception of what it means to endure pain and effort in order to achieve a greater gain in the long run. This is cognitive maturity at its utmost. In fact, she is a walking example of what good mental health is all about.

I don't know what made you choose to buy this book, but it may well be that you are suffering trauma, loss, unhappiness or stress that is making your own life miserable in some way. You probably haven't had to go through what Katie has, but what you are struggling with is serious for you, and it may well feel overwhelming at times.

I feel sure that this book will help you. You could not be in better or more motivational hands than those of Katie Piper.

Christine Webber
– psychotherapist, writer and broadcaster

Introduction

'Sometimes good things fall apart so that better things can fall together.' Marilyn Monroe

Sometimes in life the unthinkable happens. We can find ourselves in terrible situations where we feel there's no way out. Where life has thrown us a curve ball, tossing everything to chaos. You might have found out that your partner was cheating. Or been dumped, out of the blue. Lost your job. Lost a family member. Or even just feel as though you've lost your mind after suffering terrible stress. We all have personal experiences of enduring pain. Whatever your story, I hope that by sharing mine I'll help you to find hope, support and good advice.

You might already know my story. In 2008, my life changed for ever. First, I was raped by my boyfriend. Then he asked another man to throw a cup of industrial-strength sulphuric acid into my face, destroying my looks and causing terrible damage to many parts of my body. I lost half of my face as the skin melted like wax down to the bone. This was the horrendous event that led to my painfully difficult journey of recovery.

At the time I was working in London as a model and TV presenter. Just 24, ambitious and – according to the outside world – beautiful, with my blonde hair and good looks. I wasn't famous, but I wanted to be. That was my dream, but then as fast as you can snap your fingers everything was taken away...

In an instant, I was broken. Not only physically, but my spirit was crushed as well. I'd no reason to go on; I couldn't see a future, or any way out. But then somehow I learned a way to cope; and it's this step-by-step process that I went through that I'm going to share with you now.

A life-changing experience can not only rock your world but also destroy your self-esteem and spirit along the way. After I left hospital, I know that's what happened to me. I was faced with enormous challenges that I thought I couldn't handle. '*Why me?*' I asked desperately. I doubted my abilities to recover from this. At least at first. My long road to recovery involved over 200 operations to rebuild my face. I was also involved in the legal trials to get my attackers convicted. It was a lot to cope with!

My decision to make a documentary with Channel 4 was to at least try to ask people to understand why I looked the way I did. It felt like a shot in the dark at the time, but as soon as the programme had been shown, the public reaction was phenomenal.

Suddenly, instead of looking at my face and feeling pity or fear, when people looked at me they saw the face of someone they knew had survived. I was Katie Piper, 'the girl whose face was destroyed by acid' and I was called an 'inspiration'. Rather than shunning me, people in the street congratulated me for my courage. But I didn't feel like I'd done anything 'brave' (I hadn't saved anyone from a burning building!) and it was overwhelming.

Letters started arriving from all over the world, written by people from all walks of life. It wasn't just people with burns who were turning to me for help, it was also teenagers, mums, gay men, straight men; people with every problem you can imagine!

From those suffering acne, eating disorders or domestic violence, to people wanting to change gender and others consumed by feelings of inadequacy or loneliness. I was amazed. Flattered. I was also so moved by the plight of ordinary people who'd suffered so much pain – emotional and physical.

My first experience of this in person was when a stranger rushed up to me on the Tube one day. The girl's eyes were full of tears and pain. '*I just wanted to thank you for telling your story,*' she whispered. I was shocked, momentarily lost for words. Not just because a stranger had approached me, crying, but because looking into her eyes, without her having to tell me, I sensed she too had been raped. She reached out to touch my arm and then disappeared into the busy crowd, carrying her pain away, locked deep within. It was then I realised that because I had publicly acknowledged the scars on my body, other people felt able to talk to me about theirs. And not just physical scars, but also the ones they felt inside. *Invisible scars.* Somehow I'd become an ambassador not just for burns survivors, but also for people who were living with emotional pain.

Your problem matters ... because it matters to you

Whatever your problem, please don't think it's not 'big' or 'important' enough to warrant help. People so often say to me, '*But compared to your problems it's nothing,*' but actually that couldn't be further from the truth. If you cannot stop thinking about something, if you're scared or holding yourself back from doing what you want in life, or if you just feel overburdened, then it's a problem. And therefore it's important.

I once had a letter from a girl called Sarah, 24, who confessed that the big issue in her life was that she hated her tiny A-sized boobs. She never wore anything remotely tight or revealing. She avoided contact with men in case they laughed at her. Not a single day went by without her worrying about it. The snowball effect meant that she never allowed herself to get close to having a boyfriend, despite desperately wanting a relationship, and she lived alone. '*I shouldn't be complaining about this to you,*' she said. '*Not when you have as many scars as you do...*' But it is not for anyone else to judge whether your problem is worth worrying about or 'significant' enough to warrant sympathy or attention. Our natural state in life is to want to feel contentment; peace; a sense of happiness. And if that is lacking, then of course the situation is significant. But there is nothing stopping us from working towards those things when we have the right tools in place. That's where – I hope – this book will come in.

Today, the most common question that people ask me is: '*How did you manage to recover from this and remain so positive?*' And I always struggle to find an answer! How does a woman overcome a rape, a brutal attack and the loss of her whole identity? How do you get over the pain of multiple operations and start your life again, from scratch? Ultimately, how do you cope when life goes so terribly, terribly wrong?

How I got through the bad times is a question without one simple straight reply, but I hope that by writing this book I have gone some way towards answering it. Through learning just how cruel life can be, I've also learned that you *can* recover and move on to a better place. I've learned coping mechanisms and found inner strength that I never imagined I was capable of! And I promise that you can find that strength too. What I've learned above all – and it's true – is that things really *do* get better.

1

Hitting rock bottom

When you feel like you've hit the depths of despair and can't escape your pain – you've hit rock bottom. So how do you cope when all you can ask is: 'Why me?' 'Why this?' Rock bottom is an important place in anyone's recovery, and here we'll have a look at how to recognise it and how you can start to lift yourself up from it. I really know how hard this part is, but trust me, this is the start of your journey towards feeling stronger.

What is rock bottom?

Rock bottom is that dark place inside you where despair seems to have blackened every path, where you feel like you keep hitting brick walls and just don't know what else to do or where to turn. Rock bottom inevitably follows a big loss in our lives, or it can be a place we gradually sink into when things have been tough for a while without any resolution, or if we've found ourselves trapped in a cycle of self-destructive thoughts or actions. You might be feeling overwhelmed by the things that are happening, or not happening, in your life. You might have tried to think of a way out but your head is telling you that it's not possible. You might be feeling desperate and bleak about your future. You may believe that things will *never* get better and even that there's no point in going on.

Rock bottom is the worst of the worst. I know, because I've been there. It is a place where you feel no hope. No light. No point in anything. All you can think is 'nothing will get better.' When I was there, I didn't see a way out either.

It took weeks before the true reality kicked in about what had happened to my face – and my life. My first proper memory of waking up was truly terrifying. I was unable to speak, my eyelids had fused together and I couldn't breathe or swallow properly. I simply couldn't believe this was happening to me. I could hear people's voices, and I was convinced my attackers were coming back to get me. I shook constantly with fear, bracing myself for another attack as I drifted in and out of consciousness on strong painkillers. At times I awoke and presumed I must even be dead. I felt as helpless as a corpse and couldn't see how it was possible that I could ever get better, that I could ever be free from pain or terror, let alone lead an independent life. Even after the initial physical pain wore off, the feeling of despair lingered. What was going to happen to me? It was all too much to bear really. At that point, all I could do was cling on to mere survival, though at times I wasn't even sure I wanted that.

In the time it took to throw that cup of acid at me, my life had been reduced to the absolute basics. Weeks later and half blind, with a huge effort, I managed to use a pen and pad to write down a few words for my mum.

'*Am I alive?*' I scribbled. '*Help me!*'

My mum got incredibly upset by what I wrote next:

'*Kill me.*'

And at the time I truly meant it.

I'd learned I was blind. Half my face was missing. I couldn't eat. I couldn't go to the toilet by myself. I overheard a nurse telling Mum that she'd have to care for me for the rest of my life. That I'd never get fully better. That I'd never have a job or live on my own. That I'd need help for everything – even going to the loo. To my mind, I was a vegetable. There was no point in going on. I'd lost everything. I was in a place of no hope and thought I'd rather die than live like this. I decided, there and then, that as soon as I was released from hospital I'd quietly take myself off somewhere and commit suicide. After all, what was the point? This was no life. I didn't want to be a burden to my parents.

My spirit was broken. It was a dark, despairing time. Everything was black. How does a person get back from here? Or even begin to *want* to get back from there?

Twelve weeks later I was back at home, quivering like jelly. I lay on my bed while Mum made tea downstairs, and this was the first moment out of hospital I had time to think. I thought about my life and how it was today. Listing things in my head, all I could see at that point was what I'd lost.

o **My face**
The acid had reached my bones and my skin had slid off my skull and was probably placed in a medical bin at Chelsea and Westminster hospital. For any human being, your face is the first thing you present to the world. It's the first thing people look at and judge you on. It's so wrapped up with your identity, and I now couldn't bear to show my face.

o **My health**
On impact I'd breathed in and swallowed some of the acid. It had reached my oesophagus, meaning that I was now unable

to swallow and had to be fed through a tube directly into my stomach (I had to endure that for nine months). Drinking was hard too, and even breathing because I'd lost the use of my nostrils. Now I had a nose made of a piece of skin from my back, with two plastic tubes stuck up it to stop it from closing up, and I faced countless more operations.

o **My belongings**
The police had searched the flat I was sharing with five other aspiring models and presenters. I heard how they'd all fled the flat in terror of the attacker coming back for me. They'd helped me as best they could, picking up as much as they could carry in a blind panic. But it wasn't much. And once the police had taken other things for evidence, I was left with very little.

o **My career**
Obviously it was over. Completely finished.

o **All my independence, feelings of safety and any spontaneity**
Basically, everything I'd taken for granted!

Tears slipped relentlessly down my face as I thought about all of this. The reality was huge and sank into my soul like a knife, and I couldn't even cry properly because I had no eyelids to squeeze shut!

'You will get better,' Mum said, kissing my scarred forehead. 'You will get through this.' But in all honesty? I didn't think I could. After all, who the hell gets over something like this?

Getting to know rock bottom

What you feel when you are at rock bottom is individual to you, but I have talked to people in all sorts of situations, who have described their feelings in some of the following ways:

'I wished I was dead. After all, death was better than this.'

'I felt like I was in a film. One thing after another was going so badly wrong, and life was totally out of control. I was left thinking: "There is no way back from here. How can there be?"'

'I felt broken inside. I'd no idea how to put the pieces back together.'

'I didn't want to eat. Couldn't sleep. I just kept thinking over and over: "Why this? Why now?"'

'Black. Everything felt black and heavy. I couldn't stop crying even when tears stopped coming.'

'Every time I tried to think of a solution, another problem seemed to appear.'

Many of the letters I receive are from people who also feel they're at rock bottom, and I can relate so much to their words. Some have gone through terrible, horrifying, unimaginable things. Some have written after losing a relationship or their job, because of ill health or the death of a loved one, or because they feel severely depressed with no sense behind it. Many feel like they hate themselves and don't understand why. Or they feel they don't fit in at school or college and depression has set in. There are so many reasons why we hit rock bottom. It doesn't matter how we got there – all that matters is recognising that it's where we are.

Scarlett, 18, wrote to me having failed all her A levels and missed a university place after suffering from severe depression for a year. It shocked her that her future might be jeopardised, and she found it incredibly difficult to cope with her shattered dreams:

> *'When I failed all my exams, I just felt like the world had crashed. I couldn't get out of bed for days. There seemed little point.'*

Scarlett felt trapped by her circumstances and in that moment couldn't get the perspective to see that she could try again someday, and she needed to focus on dealing with her depression.

Rachel, 37, also wrote to me about hitting rock bottom when out of the blue one day her partner was violent towards her:

> *'He lost his temper. Tension had been building up for months as he had troubles at work, but when he lashed out I was so stunned, I felt unable to comprehend it. All of a sudden I had to question him, his values, my judgement, our relationship, everything. It was like I'd been living with a stranger. He'd never hit me before and now I didn't know if he'd do it again.... He'd always been so lovely. I moved out straight away and sat at my friend's house in shock for several days....'*

You may recognise these feelings of shock and hopelessness, and you may be at your own rock bottom right now. The questions and worries flooding your head may be overwhelming. This is completely understandable. But next you have to get to grips with the fact that this is now your reality, and this takes time.

Why me? Starting to understand your new life

Once you've woken up to your new reality and all the changes that have been thrown at you, the first question you'll probably ask is: 'Why me?' Many people who are facing terrible problems in their life ask this question, and it's completely understandable. It's a question said out of anger, confusion and hurt. You feel that injustice is at the root of what happened to you, and maybe it was. When bad things happen and you didn't see them coming, it's a hard pill to swallow....

What we're really saying when we ask 'Why me?' is: 'This problem doesn't belong to me! I can't manage and I don't want it!' This is a natural, normal human reaction. It's a way for our brains to cope with the shock – to momentarily separate ourselves from the problem, which at the beginning can seem so much *bigger* than we are. Take heart, though, it's a sign that you're trying to process what's happened.

Jayne, 35, wrote to me when she was diagnosed with breast cancer:

> *'I was so angry and shocked at the same time. I just thought, "It can't be right. What have I done to deserve this? Why me?" I had a small toddler to look after. It was so bloody unfair and now I had to deal with the treatment as well as being very scared. I just raged against it all and cried every night....'*

I could really relate to Jayne, as this is exactly how I felt after my attack. I thought, 'But I don't have time to deal with this, I have things to do! A life to lead!'

Simon, 27, felt the same when he was made redundant unexpectedly and could no longer be the breadwinner in his family.

'A year earlier we had proudly bought our own house. Now I couldn't afford to pay the mortgage. It wasn't just that it was frightening, it also felt so unfair. I didn't know what to do and the worry was overwhelming....'

At that moment, Simon couldn't see how to pull himself out of his problem; he was simply blind with panic that things would get worse.

I received a heartbreaking letter from 16-year-old Lisa, who was so badly bullied that she had to leave school. 'Why me?' she cried to her mum. In her letter she told me:

'The bullying just went on and on. I didn't know why. I didn't understand what it was about me that these girls wanted to pick on so much. I am a nice, kind, friendly person and I didn't deserve to be treated in such a heartless way. But they did and it was so upsetting. It made me feel worthless.'

These three examples show exactly how helpless we can feel when a devastating blow strikes. We will always struggle at first to understand why these things have happened, and this is completely understandable and a natural reaction, which we are allowed to have while we come to terms with what has changed in our lives. (To get out of rock bottom, at some point you will have to take that difficult next step – just not yet – and decide not to be a victim any longer but instead choose to be a survivor. I will talk about this in the next chapter.)

'**Despair is suffering without meaning.**'
Viktor Frankl

I love this quote. For me, it sums up what 'rock bottom' really means. When you feel such depth of pain, such confusion about why you're being made to cope with so much hardship that you simply can't imagine how it could get better or even why! When you're at rock bottom, everything feels pointless.

Psychiatrist Victor Frankl was an Auschwitz prisoner during the Second World War and suffered unimaginable cruelties at the hands of the Nazis, but somehow he found his sense of meaning. He is a complete inspiration; he proved just how powerful the human mind is, and how it can remain sane and resilient despite the most dire and desperate circumstances. After the war, Victor Frankl returned to his clinical and academic life and wrote an amazing book about his experiences called *Man's Search for Meaning*. He was a great survivor. He found that despair could teach him something. And it's true, this definitely happened to me too.

Coming out from under rock bottom

One thing you need to try to bear in mind is that you can feel like you are at rock bottom for a long time. You have a lot of healing to do and you can't really hurry yourself out of it. But in the midst of these overwhelming feelings you will gradually accept and acknowledge how bad things are, and from then on you will – very slowly – emerge from the worst of it. The truth is that our brains and bodies cannot live in such extreme anguish long-term. And the human spirit is strong, if you allow it to be.

One of the tools that helped me start to pick myself up was a mantra that I'd say over and over to myself. It went: *'I may feel absolutely awful today, but I will not always feel this way.'* Repeating this so often to myself helped to reinforce the message, and gradually I started to believe it. Mantras like this can very likely help you too, such as, *'I may have been left, but I will love and be loved again.'* Or: *'I may have lost my job, but there will be other opportunities waiting for me.'* You may not feel like these words make much sense at first, but remember the phrase 'fake it until you make it', and eventually it will start to sink in. I promise, it really works.

Letting it all out

When life is unfair, we've every right to wail and cry and be angry at the cards we've been dealt. This is actually an important step towards accepting that these unwanted changes have happened in our life. I'll talk more about acceptance later.

After the attack, I cried a river of tears and really screamed into my pillow as much as my voice at the time would allow. I was unbelievably angry, so why not? In fact, letting myself express my initial anger turned out to be *so* good for actually getting rid of it.

Though you may want to put on a brave face to protect loved ones (and of course, this *is* necessary sometimes), don't try to keep everything locked in or it will come back and bite you. When we are on our own or with others we trust, there is nothing wrong with letting rip! Head to the sanctuary of your bedroom and have a good cry. Pound your pillow with your fist, or scream under your duvet. This will physically release the emotions and start to allow you to let them out a little. On the other hand, you might be too stunned to cry. This doesn't mean you don't care. You're in shock, so just let those feelings out however you can and need to.

The power of the pen in getting out from under rock bottom

Putting pen to paper was something that I found really helpful when trying to pull myself up and out of despair. When I first returned home, my sister Suzy put a letter under my door. In it she told me how much she loved me. How important I was as her big sister. She ended it saying: *'Please, please, don't let this destroy you.'*

Her words were so powerful, and I realised how important it could be for me to write things down too. Although there was so much I couldn't do physically, writing was one thing I *could*. During the next few weeks in my bedroom, I spent hours scribbling in my journal. I don't think I'm the world's most brilliant writer, but I wrote and wrote and wrote, jotting down the first things that came into my head, whether they made sense or not.

I wrote to my parents, my attackers, my doctor, myself. Just to get all the anger, frustration and upset about life off my chest. Tears of rage and self-pity coursed down my face as I wrote. Sometimes I'd put the letters in envelopes and other times I'd rip them up. To an outsider I'd have looked like a mad woman!

As I wrote, I felt like I was in a Disney cartoon with an angel and a devil on each shoulder. I could hear the angel saying: 'There's hope,' and 'Do it for your family.' But the devil was whispering: 'Just give up.' 'You'll never look any better.' 'There's no hope.' While I wrote, I battled with both voices, and deep down I started to notice a flame inside me: a tiny flicker of hope that grew as my spirit slowly got stronger. And because of the love I received from people around me, the flames were being fanned. It gave me the space to start thinking about which mental tools I could use to help overcome my pain.

Unburdening your thoughts onto the page can be a very cathartic way of letting them out, relieving and calming your immediate feelings of anger or stress and helping you to identify any patterns in your behaviour that might not be helping. As I re-read what I'd written, even in those dark and crazy times, I could see what was rational and what was not. Having it all down on paper made it easier to see where I was being irrational and to start finding possible solutions. Even if you struggle to make sense of your writing like this, just letting your feelings out in this way can make them seem much less painful.

I recently found a letter to God that I wrote in fury while I was at rock bottom, with negative thoughts and feelings raging through my mind.

Dear God,
I hate myself. When I get dressed I don't know what to wear. I look in the mirror and see a freak, I tell myself I look okay and then I go out and get rejected. I've tried everything. I've tried being positive and I've tried to be confident. I don't want to live a life being lonely. Danny has stopped other men from being attracted to me and I feel so isolated and depressed. I hate you Danny, I hate that you've survived. You went to prison, but I've been left imprisoned alone. You have stopped there being any chance of me meeting someone else, sometimes I want you to know that, even though I know you wouldn't care.

Reading it back to myself, I saw something else – I hadn't even realised that I *had* felt like that. Just the process of writing was beginning to unpick all the trapped, crazy feelings inside my head and what a relief it was to get them out! By releasing my inner thoughts I was releasing some of the pent-up energy. The anger. The frustration. The confusion. I was even showing signs of starting to move on.

Sit in the moment, feel it and don't run away

Noticing your extreme feelings and simply sitting with them is an important step in coming to terms with big emotions. 'Live' in the moment with your pain. Some experts call this 'mindfulness' and it's about taking stock of what's happening and learning to manage your thoughts, rather than letting them take control and overwhelm you. Mindfulness won't change your situation right there and then, but it will help you to start to accept what you're going through. Sometimes, by simply allowing yourself to feel things deeply, you can notice how intense the feeling is, and also then notice how the feeling passes. This is the break-through moment when you realise that feelings, or even obsessive thoughts, *do* pass. They may only pass for a moment at first, and then start up again, but they will pass for longer and longer over time. From then on, when you start to feel awful, you will know that while you may feel terrible right at that very minute, those awful feelings won't last for ever.

I used my writing and this mindfulness technique to help me process my thoughts about how I was feeling. Here are some of the things I noticed:

o I felt hopeless (how the hell was I going to move on?)
o I felt white-hot anger (at my attackers for putting me here)
o I felt depressed (I had nothing now)
o I felt bereaved (loss of my face, career and life as I'd known it).

In a strange way, recognising these feelings and putting labels on them made everything seem less big. It meant they stopped totally consuming me. These things just became facts and it allowed me to stand back and look at my life rationally, even if just a little bit at a time.

Over the weeks, I also noticed how these feelings began to change. They weren't necessarily getting better but at least *something* was happening, when in my day-to-day life things felt pretty stuck. This gave me hope; hope that my feelings wouldn't always be this dire, and hope that other things in my life would start to change too.

The 'mindfulness' technique

When your emotions are starting to overwhelm you and you no longer feel in control of your thoughts, stop and take time out from what you're doing to practise this technique. It won't solve your problem instantly (although it will definitely make you feel a bit better), but it will help you learn to recognise these feelings and take control of them in the long term.

o Sit in your moment now. Block out everything around you and just focus on looking deep inside yourself.

The impossible can be possible: hang on to hope!

Having hope might seem like a crazy thought when you feel completely out of control of your situation, but you're wrong, I promise! Even in the depths of despair, humanity has proved that things that feel impossible *can* become possible.

We all have the resources within ourselves to cope in a crisis. Everyone. We've all heard stories of superhuman strength, such as mothers lifting up cars to rescue their children, or people with horrendous injuries surviving against all the odds. We're all capable of extraordinary things, and finding our spirit when all seems lost is no exception. Hitting rock bottom can actually be a motivator – I know it was for me.

For example, at the start of my recovery, one of the many things I found totally impossible was looking at my face in the mirror

- What are you feeling? Angry? Frustrated? Betrayed? Hopeful? Bored? Write it down. (If you don't know exactly what you're feeling, write *anything*. Just write something.)
- Now keep writing for a few minutes, as if you're spilling a stream of consciousness onto the paper. Somewhere in those sentences, something about your feelings or pain is bound to come up!
- Stop writing, come back to reality and read your words back to yourself. How do you feel reading them? Note this down too.
- Keep the paper somewhere safe, then try this exercise again in a few days or weeks and compare what you've written. Has anything changed?

without wincing, let alone liking it. But after a few months and several operations, I started to see progress and realised it was possible that it could change even more over the next year or so. This gave me at least a little bit of hope that it might get better, and I clung on to that. Each little bit of progress gave me hope for the next bit.

Things were slowly shifting, and I'd also started to *want* to stop hating myself so much. I knew I couldn't go on like this; I was getting tired of having these feelings and I felt I owed it to my supportive family and my amazing doctor, Mr Jawad, who was working so hard to help me. My perception of everything started to change.

Eventually, I got out the mirror again and, gently touching my face, tried desperately to think of any positives that had come out of this, any at all. Suddenly, a tiny thought occurred to me: with my new face and all it had been through, at least I'd never worry about wrinkles and my skin aging! I wasn't like other 24-year-old girls now, so I also didn't have to worry about the same things they did. In some bizarre way, looking like I did could be liberating!

This moment proved to me that it *is* possible to see a positive in almost any situation. Back then, that seemed quite incredible to me. And if I can do it, so can you! You really, *really* can. Remember always: your mind, spirit and the way you are thinking is what matters the most, not what is happening to you.

Let others support you when you're at rock bottom: you can't do this alone

No matter how much you think you can handle your problems on your own, or how much you think others don't want to hear what you're going through, or even if you're feeling embarrassed by the events that have got you to where you are, try to remember that those who love you generally want to help you and offer you their support – to prop you up as you go through your journey to recovery.

Someone else's shoulders to lean on will always ease your burden and encourage you to keep going. I totally believe this, and I know that if it hadn't been for the love and support of my family, my doctor and my closest friends, I would have had a much more difficult time in my recovery. Having people around us who we know care about us and want the best for us can fuel those feelings of hope – feelings that I believe we all naturally have inside of us – and can make that hope can burn brighter. Our love and respect for these people in return can be a powerful motivator to make us work even harder towards recovery.

In my charity work I've heard story after story about people who were so grateful for the encouragement and support of others. Some had wonderful families and friends, some had support from people outside their close family, such as a kind doctor, like mine. Others found solace from their pastor or a teacher, some were utterly surprised by the kindness of strangers. But what they all had in common was knowing that someone cared and was there when they needed them, and this eased the strain of going through it alone.

It's so important not to be afraid to ask for help when you need it. I'll talk more about professional help in Chapter 14 (and this may be important for you now, if you really do feel that what you're going through is too frightening to talk about with those around you), but this section is about just reaching out to those nearest to you to share what you're going through and feel their emotional and sometimes physical support. Remember, too, that people may be waiting for you to reach out to them, as many people just won't know *how* they can help you, even though they desperately want to.

You know how it is – if your friends are going through something, you may think, 'I want to help but I don't know what I can do.' So when you're going through something yourself and think you are on your own, the truth is that there are probably a lot more people than you realise who are ready and willing to prop you up – you just need to let them in. It's not about having to tell them everything that's going on in your head; it's sometimes just about having human contact, or letting them pitch in and help with any day-to-day activities you are finding tricky. Simply asking someone to sit with you, or bring you tea, or watch your kids while you go for a walk, or make you dinner if you just can't find the energy to cook for yourself: these things often make others feel so relieved that there is something they can do to help and to make you feel better.

During my darkest times, I was so angry and hurt and exhausted by what I was going through. I shouted at my poor mum. I smashed things up in my bedroom. I cried and screamed into my pillow. I shouted. 'Look at me! Just look at the state of me!' This was a desperate time. I still felt that there was so much I couldn't do. I couldn't eat properly or sleep properly

(I had terrible nightmares), I couldn't leave the house, I faced visits from the police to talk about the terrifying prospect of the trial of my attackers, not to mention the painful on-going hospital treatments I was enduring. I felt like my world had not only changed overnight, but that it had become like a living hell. I didn't know which way to turn or what to do to feel better. I didn't even want to try and feel better.

But when I was contemplating death, I realised how many people around me were willing me to get better. They were cheerleading for me to dig deep and survive. They cared. They really did. Little by little, I let them in and allowed them to help me, and they were so wonderful. Without these supportive people, I would have had a considerably more difficult time and may have even felt like giving up, but how could I give up when every day I heard those familiar voices around me, full of love and willing me on? How could I turn my back and long for death when they were full of hope for a good life ahead? This was one of the first of many glimmers which pulled me through. Mum kept listening quietly, Dad tried to keep my spirits up with humour, my brother and sister told me how much they loved me. If you let them, your friends, family and other people from your support network can and will do the same.

Everyone has someone they can turn to, even if they have to look a little harder for it than I did. I know I was lucky, but if you look, you will find people who will be kind, supportive and encouraging and who will just listen – you may not realise who they are right at this very minute, but keep your eyes and ears open and you will notice kindness around you. And if nothing else, please remember that I believe in you. I really do. And I know that you have the strength within to get through.

The Samaritans

If you're feeling in need of urgent help and support, or feel suicidal and that you have nowhere or no one to turn to, please, please call The Samaritans.

This amazing organisation offers people emotional support 24 hours a day, including to those who feel they cannot go on for a second longer. You can get in touch by email, letter, on the telephone or face to face. The most common reasons people ring them are over relationship problems, a big loss (e.g. a job or bereavement), work or college stress and body issues, but whatever your problem is, they will listen. And they listen for as long as you need, even if it's for a couple of hours.

You can contact them on: **08457 909090**, or if you feel unable even to talk about it, email: **jo@samaritans.org** or write to them: Chris, PO Box 90 90, Stirling, FK8 2SA.

I'll talk later about all kinds of therapy and other organisations who can help you, but if your feelings are out of control *right now* and you just need to connect with another caring human being – the Samaritans are there to listen to you.

Some points to remember in your dark early days:

o **When the worst happens, remember you're in shock and let people help you.** Please don't try to deal with your crisis all alone. Remember that many people love you – and they want to help. Even if you don't want to talk, let people sit with you. Sometimes it's really reassuring just to have someone else in the same room.

o **If friends or family ask how they can help, tell them.** Even if it's just something practical, like: 'Could you make me a cup of tea?' or 'Could you pick up the kids from school and look after them for a bit?' And don't be embarrassed to go back to your parents. When we are distressed, most parents are quick to cuddle and cosset us. It makes them feel helpful and valuable to be able to care for us like they did when we were children. This can be very comforting for us and them.

o **Don't be afraid to pick up the phone and call someone close when you are feeling bad.** You'd hope they'd do the same, wouldn't you?

o **Treat yourself with great kindness and care.** It's all too easy to hide away and stop looking after yourself when you're feeling hideous. Do little things for yourself: make yourself have long scented baths or listen to music that means something to you. Get plenty of sleep, keep warm and don't forget to eat well. This may all sound obvious, but these basics are often the first things to get neglected when we're in crisis.

o **Go easy on the alcohol.** It's a depressant and won't make you feel any better.

o **Remember that rock bottom is only a feeling – it is not a fact!** Do everything you can to hang on to the knowledge and belief that life will go on and that you will get over this. There *is* life on the other side of the pain.

o **Sit in the moment and just acknowledge your painful feelings.** This can give you some comfort, and will help you to manage your emotions.

o **Try writing things down.** Putting things on paper can really help you work through them.

CHAPTER 2

Be a survivor, not a victim

When you're coming to grips with rock bottom, the very next step towards recovery is deciding whether to see yourself as a victim or a survivor. By 'victim' I don't mean the definition of someone who has been on the receiving end of something terrible (for example, what happened to me – I was the victim of a horrible crime). By 'victim', here I mean someone who always identifies themselves by what happened to them. A survivor, on the other hand, is someone who has been through something terrible and finds new life on the other side. The survivor moves forward and accepts what's happened, a victim wallows and stays stuck. And the difference between being one or the other is all in your mind. It really is a choice, and I hope you'll choose to survive!

Making a conscious decision to want to recover and be free of pain

Have you ever heard a friend or relative say, 'It's *never* going to get better,' 'I *can't* go on,' or 'I *don't* see a way out'? Does this negative language sound familiar? If so, you'll know how this makes you worry that perhaps they actually *won't* recover – at least, not while they are thinking and speaking like this. Often this is how someone will feel in the early days after a devastating change to their life, which is to be expected – as I talked about in the last chapter – but if they continue to feel this way as time passes, it will make it more difficult for them to recover and move on.

It's easy for those on the outside to see that you are jeopardising your recovery with negative thinking, but as you know, it's so much harder to deal with these feelings on the inside. There are so many fears people have within themselves, and so many reasons why problems might seem unbearable. But when we're faced with major difficulties, there are *always* small changes we can make to help us feel more positive and lead to more hopeful times – if we look hard enough. Even if you feel so bleak that you can see no way out, it's vital to at least *want* things to get better. And that's the first step to becoming a survivor.

Asking yourself: 'Am I a victim or a survivor?'

After my attack, I certainly felt like a victim. I didn't recognise my own reflection, I was disfigured, had flashbacks and nightmares and couldn't leave the house. I had to face my attackers in the courts, so even in the eyes of the law I was the victim. With all these things going on, how could I *not* feel like a victim?

But deep down I knew I didn't want to be labelled forever as the 'acid-attack girl' whose life had been ruined and who became a recluse. Even in the early days I started to feel bored and trapped sitting around at home. Even though I felt all my dreams were over, I didn't want this kind of hidden-away life, I didn't want this to become my reality. That was when the penny dropped.

Suddenly I realised that I WANTED to be a survivor. I wanted to be the girl who got on with her life and didn't crumble, even after something so awful. Even if I didn't know *how* I'd do it, the will inside me for things to change for the better was so strong. Little did I know it at the time, but just by making this conscious decision that I wanted to recover, I was already halfway there.

For me, an important step in no longer seeing myself as a victim was in changing my view and starting to see my attackers as the victims instead. Through letters I wrote to them (which I later destroyed), I began to realise that they were in prison, awaiting trial, with their liberty taken away, whereas I was free. Okay, I was still stuck at home, but I could go out in the car, I could do whatever I liked in the house and I could dream of one day moving on from this.

I told myself over and over again that they'd hurt my face, but that was *all*. I tried to redirect the anger I felt towards them so that I could be the victor in all this mess. I so badly didn't want to be stuck at home for ever. I so badly didn't want to spend my life feeling full of bitterness. So every day I woke up and thought again: '*They* are the victims. *I* am the survivor.' I said it out loud, I wrote it down, I talked about these thoughts with my family until, finally, I started to believe it.

I realised that if I railed against the world and life and got stuck in victimhood, refusing to accept the cards I'd been dealt, the journey ahead would be *more* painful. I didn't want to end up wallowing.

Another big step for me was deciding never ever to refer to myself as a 'burns victim' again. Instead, I started saying, 'I'm a survivor.' Domestic-violence charities often refer to their clients as domestic violence 'survivors' – for a similar reason. Only survivors survive! If you refuse to be a victim, things will shift. Even if you don't necessarily believe they will at first.

I recently met two sisters, who both suffered a similar trauma and who told me their stories. It really shows the difference between thinking of ourselves in terms of 'victim' or 'survivor'. Tracy, 26, and her sister Maeve, 28, were in a frightening train crash. Their physical injuries were about the same, but Maeve found it harder to overcome the experience. 'I don't dare to get on a train again,' she said. 'It's just too risky.' She stayed at home, off work, far longer than Tracy did, and then found it traumatic to get back to her job and everyday life. She preferred to lock herself away at home where she felt nothing bad could happen to her.

Meanwhile, after spending a period in shock, her sister Tracy decided to tackle her fears head-on and went to see a therapist to help sort out her thoughts and feelings. She also talked to her friends and decided to travel on a train again as soon as possible. She openly talked about putting the events of the crash behind her and getting control of her life.

Maeve really did suffer from the crash, but she never spoke about recovery apart from saying she didn't *expect* to recover, which just fuelled her fears, and today she's still terrified of being hurt again. Tracy, however, admitted that she had been very scared too, but she was determined not to let it get the better of her, and made positive steps towards regaining control of her life. The difference between how Maeve and Tracy handled their initial thoughts was a great predictor for their end result. Of course, it's never too late for Maeve to overcome what has happened to her, but first she must choose that she wants to, and only then will the recovery follow.

Recovering from a trauma or upset is hard, of course. Our hearts should always go out to those suffering and we should always show compassion, but there is a clear difference between wanting to recover and being positive, compared to sliding into victimhood and not willing yourself to move forward – and we should remember this.

Survivor speak

To go from being a victim to a survivor you need to change your approach and turn negatives into positives, and this starts with the way you think and talk about your situation.

Things a victim says:
'Why me?'
'It's not fair.'
'I don't deserve this.'
'I can't deal with this.'
'I hate my life and how it's turned out.'
'There's nothing I can do.'

Things a survivor says:
'I can overcome this.'
'I will make the best of this, whatever that is.'
'I will prove them wrong.'
'This too will pass.'
'I am going to play this hand dealt to me.'
'I know I won't always feel like this.'

Stop predicting the worst

Many people who go through terrible times say things like: 'I will never get another job.' Or: 'No one else will ever love me and I will be lonely for ever.' Or: 'It's all bound to go downhill from here.' But one thing I quickly learned was not to overload my unhappiness by making predictions for a horrible future.

Someone once said to me: 'You don't have a crystal ball, so you can't possibly know what will or won't happen to you.' And she was right! Torturing yourself with these negative thoughts is totally unproductive. If you find yourself having flashbacks or repeating cycles of negativity, that's when you need to seek further help (we'll talk about that more later on).

Even if you don't feel like you're going to recover, talk as if you are. This isn't always easy – of course it isn't! – but if you actively say that things will get better and use language that reinforces this ('I *will* recover from this'; 'I *will* love again'; 'I *will* have a healthy relationship with food'), things are far more likely to hurry up and get better. Remind yourself of all the things you'd like to change and improve. Write them down. Then openly talk about them with friends. Put them out there in the universe! This is the kind of thinking that survivors do – they use all their will to make things happen. We'll look more at the power of positivity in Chapter 5.

Deep within – find your spirit!

We all have spirit. It's the thing that makes us fight for what we believe in. It makes us feisty. It makes us leap towards the things we want to do, and keeps us focused on getting them. But sometimes, when our lives have taken a wrong turn, our spirit feels lost or broken. Believing that you're a survivor is the first step towards strengthening your damaged spirit and letting it thrive!

Even when my spirit felt broken, sometimes I saw a flicker of my old, stubborn, determined self, and when I felt it, I just let it flourish. If nothing else, it made me feel more alive and connected to the world. I tried to listen to the voice inside me that said: 'You *will* be okay.'

Maybe it's just me, but if I'm told I cannot do something, that's when I want to prove everyone wrong. In hospital some of the doctors were brutal with their prognosis. There was so much uncertainty about my recovery, and none of it looked good: 'We don't know if you'll be able to swallow normally again.' 'We don't know if your eyesight will recover.' 'Your eyelids will never work.' 'We don't know if the skin grafts will be successful.'

'Oh great!' I thought. 'I won't be able to see or eat properly *and* I'll never look the same again.' When I overheard the nurses tell Mum: 'You'll always have to be her carer now,' my heart sank. I mean, my mum is one of my biggest heroes but nobody wants to have to be looked after 24 hours a day, and even taken to the toilet.

'No way!' I thought. 'I love Mum to bits but that would drive me crazy!' I wanted to be her grown-up daughter, not her baby again. Looking back, this was quite an amusing thought and proved to me, even amongst all this madness, that I still felt a sense of normality too.

A tiny voice inside me was saying, 'No, you're wrong. I will show you,' and instead of ignoring it, I chose to turn up the volume. And this is my best advice to you: when you feel a little glimmer of hope inside or are able to see very briefly the light at the end of the tunnel, immediately make that voice or thought LOUDER!

Listen to the positive voice inside you

This simple exercise can help you to be a survivor and begin to see your circumstances in a different, more positive, light. Answer the questions below, write down your answers and see what you discover. Try really hard to think of positive things to say, even if they seem trivial or you feel like you're clutching at straws.

o Think about the events and feelings that have happened to you. Can you find anything positive in your situation, anything at all, even if it's tiny?

o Describe your experiences out loud to yourself, or write them down. Notice the language you use, both out loud/on paper, as well as the thoughts going through your head at the same time. Is the language positive or negative? Do you say things like 'can't' and 'won't', or 'can' and 'will'? Are you talking mostly about the past or about the future? Are yours the words of a victim or a survivor?

o What have you learned from your experiences? Are there any lessons you can take from them or that you would want to pass on to other people?

o What are you going to tell people about your situation in 10 years' time?

o If somebody else was in your situation, what advice would you give them, or how would you try to help?

There is an obvious difference between acting as a victim and acting as a survivor. Survivors find positive answers to questions like these. Work out what they are for *your* situation. If you can't find them today, come back another time and try again. I know you will find them eventually.

Escaping the pitfalls of victimhood: bitterness and wallowing

Beware of the two enemies of 'survivor thinking': bitterness and wallowing – they're all too easy to indulge in. Wallowing is when you get stuck in patterns of negative thinking that you can't get out of (or sometimes don't want to get out of), and bitterness is when you turn your anger and resentment against the world for what you're going through.

I do believe that a little wallowing is okay, especially when you're working your way through your initial feelings, but it can easily become a self-destructive habit and can cause you to get stuck in the past. Bitterness is a knock-on effect from wallowing. Your wallowing keeps you going round in circles in your head until you start to view the world as an outsider and with envy. It is a poison that makes you feel unable to share in other people's happiness because you're so stuck in your own unhappiness. We try to use bitterness to protect ourselves from feeling further hurt, but in truth, we're only hurting ourselves more by denying ourselves any joy. Bitterness will only cut you off from the very things and people who can help you.

So, how do you recognise wallowing? It can be hard to identify the cut-off point at which you move from processing your feelings into full-blown wallowing, but here are some pointers that should help:

o Notice if you're going round in circles. Are you continually stuck repeating the same negative thoughts or feelings, in your head, or to others? In return, you may notice that your loved ones are also starting to repeat themselves when addressing your concerns.

o Have you started to identify yourself using your problem? Do you think of yourself as the person who had an accident; the abandoned wife; the misunderstood friend?

o Are you unable (or unwilling) to see any opportunities for moving away from this type of feeling?

I was sent a letter by a woman who had been injured as a child twenty years before, when she dived into the shallow end of a swimming pool, leaving her arm paralysed and her school-life terribly difficult due to bullying. Although her physical pain was minimal now, emotionally she couldn't move on. She was a lovely, kind person, but grew up feeling defined by her disability, and as a result she can't remember a time when she didn't feel 'different'. She felt that her accident had crushed any spirit. She has replayed the scene of the accident in her mind a thousand times, as if by doing so she could undo the events. And sadly, really sadly for her, it's led to a life of victimhood and wallowing. By remaining stuck in the past, she's been unable to make a future for herself. She resented the good things that were happening to those around her, and constantly felt the unfairness that her life was terrible compared to the lives of others, though she did very little to actually find her own happiness. This is such a common thing, which I hear all the time, and it breaks my heart because I know it's bitterness that has put a great big wall around these people, and I know that this wall *can* come down.

Sometimes it can be hard to get perspective and see wallowing and bitterness in yourself. But if you've lived with the same negative thoughts and feelings for years, if your friends and family have hinted that it's time to move forward or that you may be unfair in your thinking towards others, if you think too much about your past, or if you feel every day that your problems are permanent and that nobody could ever understand, then you may very well be stuck in the wallowing/bitterness cycle.

Take the example of Bridget, 22, who was cheated on by her partner. She felt that she couldn't move on and that her life was changed for ever as a result. She'd already been through the grieving process, crying and mourning the loss of her boyfriend. But yet she still felt stuck there.

'I watched your documentary and was overwhelmed with admiration about not only the courage you showed but also the way you moved on. I wish it was as easy for me. This isn't the same sort of problem, but I was dumped by my boyfriend of a year when I was 18, three years ago. We were together for a year but towards the end I discovered he'd been cheating on me the whole time. I was so upset, I cut my wrists. I couldn't believe he had betrayed me like that. I loved him so much. Now, three years on, I still think about him every day. I feel so sad still and can't face dating other guys, and I feel so jealous of my friends with boyfriends. How do I move on from this?'

Like so many who suffer heartbreak, Bridget is stuck replaying the scenes of her relationship over and over. It is so easy to do this when a terrible, life-changing event has knocked your self-esteem. It's even clouded her view of other friends' lives. But there is a way forward from here.

Moving on – putting the past behind you to make way for the future

Like deciding to be a survivor, moving on is also a conscious decision. It's something you have to want to do. Wallowing in the past simply ruins your future. Grieving (and that can be about anything from a job loss to a bereavement to wishing for your old life back) is a natural process and the timescale varies, but there comes a time when it's important to ask who it is you're hurting by not getting past this problem. If you're brave and honest with yourself, you'll realise that the answer is 'you'. But haven't you already suffered enough? With some effort and help you can and will start enjoying life again, so now is the time to decide that this is what you want and take responsibility for making it happen.

Your life is what you decide to make it

All too often in life, we wait for good things to happen to us or hope that bad things will simply go away. What we tend to overlook is that what happens in our lives is almost entirely down to our own actions and thoughts. Taking responsibility for your life is so empowering! You may feel like the victim in some things and you may *actually* have been a victim at one point, but now it's time to make the decision to own your life, to be the survivor you are, and part of that is learning from the things that went wrong so you can be stronger for the future. Your actions may have been part of the problem, but the good news is that your actions can also be part of the solution.

Sometimes it's all too easy to not take responsibility, allowing yourself to rely on other people completely. The more you take control of your own life, the more secure you will feel. The other benefit is that those around you will respect you for having things in your life that are truly yours and for following your dreams, and you will attract people who nurture you to follow your dreams.

After I got home from hospital, I'd joke with Mum sometimes when she asked me to put my washing away. 'I can't Mum,' I'd tease. 'I am blind!'

But we both knew that if I was able to joke about it, it was time for me to pitch in. So I started to make more of an effort and help around the house. I knew that I eventually wanted to live by myself and be independent again, so this was one way of taking responsibility and proving to myself that it was possible, even if it meant doing all the boring stuff again!

Some people avoid taking responsibility for their own lives because they fear making their own choices. They feel they need someone else in their life for validation, to make them feel worthy. We all know the girl who changes everything in her life for a new boyfriend, the one who changes her whole identity and ignores her own life once she has someone new. Maybe that girl is you? If we live our lives for others, we don't build a strong sense of self. But know this: if you need someone else to make you a whole person, you'll waste so much time in fear that they'll leave you. If you have things in your life that you work hard at and which fulfil you, then you will be far more relaxed in your relationships, and will likely be a better partner or friend and probably less 'needy' as a result too.

Accepting your situation is the first step towards taking responsibility for your life

One definite fact is that the sooner you accept what's happened in your life, whatever it may be, the faster you will recover and move on. This may seem easier said than done and it doesn't mean you have to like what's going on, but it's an important challenge and one of the things that helped me most in the early stages of my recovery.

In my case, the only way I could move on with my life was if I stopped asking myself 'Why has this happened?' and instead asked 'How can I recover?' Most of the 'whys' that we ask ourselves in life are vague questions for which we'll never get answers! Life is not simple. Situations and other people's motivations – and even our own motivations – are all very complex. So sometimes it is better not to look for answers, or make the 'Why?' a problem in our lives, but simply to accept what has happened in the past and try to look forward to a different future in a positive way. That is surviving, that is refusing to be a victim.

If I hadn't accepted my situation, I would have been stuck on a treadmill of misery, and I knew I didn't want that! It didn't mean I had to like my situation, it just meant that I had to accept that I couldn't bring back my old self, my old life, my old face. It was, and is, a simple fact. And by allowing myself to accept this, I could start to build on and believe in my *new* self, my *new* life, my *new* face.

Therapists I've spoken to have told me that people rarely make progress until they've really accepted the situation in which they find themselves. One counsellor, who deals with a lot of people who have been rejected in relationships, says they initially believe things like: 'I'm sure he's made a mistake and will come back.' Or: 'She'll find she needs me and can't manage on her own.' Apparently, it's only when they stop denying what's happened and accept the truth that they begin to deal with the horrible pain that goes with that truth, and then they begin to recover.

You can't move on if you don't take a deep breath and think: 'Okay, so I didn't want this to happen, but it *has* happened. Now what do I need to do next?' If you don't ask what comes next, then, simply put, your situation will stay the same. Of course, the reasons for not asking ourselves 'What next?' are completely understandable – letting go of the past and facing an unknown future is scary! But instead of overwhelming yourself and trying to imagine everything that lies ahead, all at once, just live in the moment with a feeling of acceptance. That's as far as you need to go right now.

You may have heard about the 'stages of grief', and one of these is acceptance. It's merely the understanding that life does go on, even if it feels like it shouldn't and that you want to bottle and protect what you've lost, to honour and love what came before for fear that you will forget those happy feelings from the past. But you won't forget those feelings, or those people, or those happy times you had. They are part of you. But if you resist acceptance, you will be stopping a natural healing process.

One factor that helped me to accept my new situation was, ironically, fear! (I'll talk more about fear in Chapter 6). I was scared of ending up a bitter, broken person. I didn't want to stay hidden at home. I didn't want my attackers to have succeeded in destroying me.

As part of my move towards acceptance I looked around and thought: 'Okay, this is what I am left with. I don't wish to die, so how can I live with this?' One way I did this was to tell myself, 'I'm a different person now.' Although I still had the same personality, I grew to understand that for my own sanity, I couldn't even try to live my life like the 'old' Katie. I had to face facts that I was no longer the pretty, bubbly blonde, that I couldn't be a model or TV presenter or compare myself to my peers. I was on a very different journey and I had to accept this.

People ask me if I can still look at old pictures of myself and yes, now I can. I look at them and smile as if looking at an old friend. It took a while, but it's something I feel completely okay with now because I've accepted my new self. When I look back at the old Katie, I feel glad I knew her. I'm glad she made the most of her life back then. The raw grief of losing her has gone, and I've worked hard not to feel bitterness, so I'm able to look at the photos in a fond way. 'She was lovely,' I think. Because 'she' has gone and I've accepted that. Sometimes I've even joked it's a bit like an old lady looking at snaps of herself thinking: 'Ooh, wasn't I a looker back then?!' It feels good to be in a place where I can laugh about it. It helps reinforce to me that I have accepted it.

Put it into words

One of the ways I worked through my acceptance was by writing letters and poems about learning to love my new face. This poem is about leaving my old face behind. Reading it now, I'm surprised at how incredibly forgiving it is, showing how at the time I was slowly coming to terms with what happened.

Why don't you try writing a poem or letter to yourself, accepting what has happened or is happening? Or write down all the ways in which you now see life differently, or even try and find things that might be better about your life now. When I wrote this poem, I was in a terrible place, but I challenged myself to remember the good times and think of my face with kindness.

Katie: My Old Face

I miss you.
I think about you every day.
The fun we used to have, those memories I have of you,
I will always treasure.
I know, I know you are gone for ever (but never forgotten).
We were crazy together and I am glad, we really made the most of it.
I find it hard to think about the fact you don't exist in this world
*   any more.*
So strange.
Sometimes I wonder if we will be reunited in Heaven?
I took care of you, all those expensive creams, if I close my eyes I can
*   picture and feel all the contours as I would rub the face cream on,*
*   the flat wide nose, the perfect cupid's bow. I spent so much time*
*   perfecting those brows!*
I'm sorry I sometimes put you through the sunbed, that horrifies
*   me now!*
You'd be shocked, I've really changed. I'm kind to this face and I love it,
*   but nothing will replace you. Sometimes I'm too hard on this face.*
If I had one wish I would see you again, for one day, wear you
*   again, I would take you to the supermarket and walk you around,*
*   smiling, greeting everyone,*
I'm sorry I let you down and let him take you away.
I will never destroy your pictures. I'm scared as you fade in my mind
*   and I accept this face more. But I'm sorry it's the way it must be*
*   until we meet again. x*

Getting to where you want to be, one day at a time

When we're trying to make positive changes to the things that are really bugging us in our lives – like losing weight, quitting smoking, getting rid of an unhealthy relationship or following your dreams to start a new career – it's easy to race ahead with fears and negativity and see it all as too much hard and painful work.

If you wake up in the morning and think: 'Oh god, I've got sooo much to cope with!' and you worry about what the day, the week, the next month or years will bring, it's enough to scare anyone. Just after my attack, even coping with the things I had to do in a single day was terrifying and felt like torture.

So, when those overwhelming feelings come up, just stop for a minute and breathe. The past and the future are not here right now. But you are. And all you have to do is get through the day. And even if a day seems overwhelming, then all you need to deal with is the next hour, or even the next five minutes, and don't think about what comes next until it comes.

Breaking down what needs to be done into manageable chunks of time or achievable tasks instantly makes it easier. It may seem impossible now to go the rest of your life without smoking, but you can probably go five minutes! You may want to eat the entire contents of your fridge, but if you cut out one unhealthy thing from your next meal and replace it with something healthy, then that's one less unhealthy thing than you ate at your last meal. You may feel smothered by feelings that you'll never love someone as much as the one who left you, but you can probably find a way to smile at a nice-looking person! Just making a small step towards what you want will motivate you enormously towards the next step. The same goes for the harder things we go through, like losing loved ones. If you can get through today, tomorrow will be easier.

Shifting your motivation can help too. After the attack, my motivation had to move from chasing the next modelling job to mere survival. I'd woken from my coma, next I had to learn to walk again and focus on building my strength. If I'd thought about the whole picture at once, I would have freaked out. So I just worked towards tiny goals at first. I had no nose or eyelids. I had to focus on regaining those body parts before I could even dream of a day when I could wear makeup again or go shopping or lead an independent life, let alone start a charity and lead the life I have now. If I hadn't begun small, focusing on my nose and eyelids, and all those basic things I had to do and recover from, I wouldn't have moved to the next step and I certainly wouldn't be where I am now.

My friend Louise was in an unhealthy relationship that she'd spent ages trying to end. Time and again she ditched her unreliable and untrustworthy boyfriend only to keep running back (even though he had cheated on her a few times). Poor Louise had terrible self-esteem issues and was afraid to let him go; she was afraid of what might happen to her if she left him, and she was flooded with worry and fear that she would never find anyone else to love her, or that he would find someone else. Eventually she worked up the nerve to break up with him and even deleted his number. But she still had his email address and found it really hard to resist sending him a message. So, for the first few days, after every hour she went without contacting him, she told herself: 'Well done!' When the urge to ring him was overwhelming, she would ring one of her friends instead. Very slowly, after a week, she found herself not even thinking about him for a whole half hour, then an hour, then a couple of hours. Two months passed, and she found herself going whole days with barely a thought of him. She felt so relieved! This would have felt impossible to begin with, if she'd not broken up the days into those first raw hours and taken it one step at a time.

Sticking to a routine can also help get us through the difficult days, by giving us a reassuringly solid base with expected events to break down the day. You might not feel like eating, but at least stop for a snack at lunchtime anyway. Always set your alarm for the same time each morning. Our bodies, as well as our minds, like routine, and it means you can give yourself goals – you can say things like, 'I made it all the way until lunch without doing X' (as long as your goals are healthy!). We are creatures of habit and your positive actions can become habits too.

> **'Things will never get better if you believe they won't.'** Anon.

Rewarding yourself

This might sound like the last thing you want to do when you're feeling miserable or worthless, but when you're down in the dumps, please try to treat yourself to at least one nice thing a day. Doing something nice needn't involve spending money: it could just be speaking to your best friend before you go to bed, or getting some fresh air in your local park, or re-potting a plant and putting it on the windowsill where you can enjoy it. However you treat yourself, it simply shows you that you're worth it. Which you are!

And don't forget to congratulate yourself at the end of each day. If you're in 'one day at a time' mode, you deserve it! Even if you haven't reached all your goals, stay positive – think: 'I may not have done everything I wanted to today, or maybe it went a bit wrong, but I still deserve something nice because I'm a good person, because I want my life to be better and I'm working hard to get there.'

Positive progress

To help me along with my small steps, my dad started taking photos of my recovery. At first I wasn't sure about this. After all, why would I want pictures of myself looking like I did in this state? To begin with, I didn't want to look at the photos; they just made me feel upset. But small improvements were being made every week, and as my many operations took place, bit by bit I slowly started to look better. Of course, there were some backwards steps but generally my progress was positive. Having photos to compare really proved this and the photo diary became a huge part of my emotional recovery. It turned out to be incredibly motivating! Every week things were changing, things were getting better and now I could look back and see exactly how. I had solid proof that the treatments were working. This really empowered me!

Choosing to be a survivor: points to remember

o **To become a survivor, you have to *want* to be one.** Make a conscious decision to choose survival over victimhood and work hard to behave like a survivor in every way you can.

o **Choose your words carefully.** Survivors speak in positives, telling themselves that they 'can' do things and 'will' recover. Don't fall into the 'can't' and 'won't' trap, or you'll be speaking like a victim. Asking 'How?' instead of 'Why?' helps you to look forward and take action instead of gazing backwards into your past.

o **Talk the positive talk.** Even if you feel like it's all a big pretence, talk as if you will recover, predict good things for yourself and will them to be true. Just saying these things out loud can often get the ball rolling, and if you say them often enough you'll start to believe them.

o **Look for positives in everything,** no matter how unimportant or trivial the positive aspects seem. Pinpointing the positives – however tiny – will help you see your circumstances in a new light and make the most of your situation.

o **Wallowing and bitterness are the two enemies of survival and recovery.** Pay attention so you don't end up there! Recognise and steer clear of circular or negative patterns.

o **Accepting your situation gives you strength to start moving on.** If you don't accept what has happened, you'll just stay stuck. It's a natural healing process, so give yourself time to accept your situation and start getting used to the new feelings you're having. Only then can you start to look at how you're going to move on and begin to recognise what will make you feel better. And you'll be moving forward as a survivor!

o **You only have to get through one day at a time.** Nothing more. Keep your goals small and break things down into tiny steps. And please don't forget to reward yourself.

CHAPTER 3

Counting your blessings

We are all blessed with good things in our lives, but sometimes we take these for granted when all we can see are the hurtful things happening to us. Gratitude is important for taking stock of our situation, and a powerful tool to help change our perspective for the better. Even in our darkest times we need to count our blessings; it can be a great motivator for healing. When I lost my face, I had to work hard to be grateful for what I had left, but when I did, everything started to change for the better.

Taking a moment to be grateful

It's so often not until things go wrong that we recognise all the wonderful things we have in our lives. And even then, we sometimes focus only on what we've lost rather than what we still have.

Before my attack, I took for granted all the things that so many of us do, like my family (I didn't keep in contact with my mum and dad very much; I was having too much fun in London), my looks and having a healthy body (I used to eat badly to lose weight and push myself to the limits, drinking or smoking, not worrying about how it would affect me in the long term). I had no reason to think anything bad would ever happen to me. After my attack, suddenly these things became precious and I couldn't believe that I ever had taken them for granted.

'Count your blessings' may sound like something your granny might tell you to do, but actually scientists and psychologists (people in the know!) are now telling us to do it – because they say that in doing so we can see all we value and have to protect in our lives and therefore take responsibility for our own happiness and become more optimistic people – if we work at it. It makes sense. If we honour the things in life that are important to us, the less likely we will be to have regrets in the future (like wishing we'd called our parents more when they're gone).

Many therapists get their clients to list the happy things that have happened in their week instead of merely focusing on the sad and miserable ones. I am all for doing this. It can really massively change your whole perspective. We can all moan about what we *don't* have, but what about celebrating the things we *do*? There is a top psychiatrist in Italy – Professor Giovanni Fava – who encourages his patients to keep a 'happiness diary'. He says that once people write down the details of positive moments, happy feelings really take root in their minds. By *choosing* to focus on what's good, and by telling ourselves something consciously, it affects our subconscious. In other words, the happiness starts to sink in and become a part of us.

Being aware of and grateful for happy moments, and the good things that happen in our lives, is something we can all do. And if we start to get into the habit of looking for these good moments every day, rather than listing all the stuff that has got us down, we can definitely become more positive and happy. Sounds good to me! Try and do it at the end of every day. Here's something I recently wrote down:

Today I woke up to find the sun was shining. I feel grateful for the good memories of last night when my friend cooked me a meal. I was glad my sister rang for a chat and it felt good to speak to Mum, too, to tell her about my day. I was even happy to see a favourite programme of mine on TV, and for the biscuits I had in my cupboard for a treat after dinner!

These were the things that had made me happy on that particular day. Of course, frustrating things had also happened – the Tube was late, I left my purse at home and had to go back and get it – but I didn't write those down, as this was just about looking at the good things. In fact, it even made me forget the irritating parts of my day.

Some of the experts who are doing research into happiness believe that contented humans live longer than those who feel miserable, and that happy people are much more likely to form fulfilling romantic relationships. I'm sure if you look at the people around you, you'll see that's true, and maybe even obvious! I know from my own experience that you can take responsibility for your own happiness. It takes time, but since I learned this I feel like I can conquer anything. So what are you waiting for? Start listing the things that make you grateful and happy!

Cherish the small things

When things were at their very worst, when all seemed lost, I would work hard to think to myself: at least I am not blind in *both* eyes; at least my attackers are in prison now; at least I live in a country where such an act is a crime and where we have excellent medical care; at least I am alive.

Just being grateful for the very small, tiny plus-points is all you need to get started. There is always, always someone worse off than you and whose suffering is greater. Of course, that doesn't mean you're not suffering too, and as I said in my introduction, your problems are unique and important to you. But at the same time you just need to keep it in perspective that, even when you think you've lost everything (as I certainly thought right after my attack), you probably haven't – so do everything to cling to what you *do* have and take it from there.

'If we all threw our problems in a pile and saw everyone else's, we'd grab ours back.' Regina Brett, Pulitzer Prize nominee and breast-cancer survivor

One defining moment for me was when I was at the specialist burns rehabilitation centre in France. For a year I'd been in hospital or stuck at home. I'd hardly been outside and even then had only really gone from the car to hospital to my parents' house and back again. My senses had been consumed by the whir of hospital machines during operations or the sounds of the fridge and TV in my parents' house. I hadn't experienced the basics of fresh air and nature for a very long time.

On my first day in France, I went for a walk by myself in the village. I found a bench and for a few minutes just sat, closed my eyes and heard the sound of trees rustling and birds tweeting. The sense of peace was overwhelming. For the first time in ages I felt truly alive and part of the world again. (Nature has an amazing ability to do this!) I felt free, optimistic, healthy and truly able to count my blessings.

I was a 24-year-old who previously thought I was happiest in noisy clubs and bars, and would never have imagined feeling so content hearing the outside world. But I was, and it made me realise that it's the tiny things that count. I was so grateful to feel the sun on my face, to hear birds instead of machines, to know I was free and could enjoy a moment of peace in the fresh air. Of course, I was still going through so much, but it didn't mean I couldn't feel great joy too. I ran back to my room, called my mum and told her how excited I was. She cried with happiness too, because she knew I was noticing the beauty in the world instead of all the sorrow I had experienced.

Through my charity work I met a 40-year-old man named Mike who knows this feeling well and understands how our gratitude can intensify after we've been through something tough:

> *'I was made redundant in the recession and it was a huge shock to the system. I'd gone from being a successful businessman to being at home every single day. We even lost our house as I couldn't pay the mortgage. But then I started to spend more time with my kids, then aged 3, 6 and 8. And I realised I had been so busy that I had missed so much of their lives. We found somewhere smaller to live, and we were suddenly in each other's lives so much more. It was strange at first but I started to enjoy it. I felt I'd taken them for granted before, and in this world of change, they became my stability. I'd never felt so lucky to be a dad.'*

Mike is an example of learning to appreciate now what you might regret having taken for granted later. He realised that his redundancy was actually something to be grateful for, as it meant that he wouldn't later look back on his life and wish he had spent more time with his children. It focused him on the important things in his life and reminded him that while things like a big house or a lot of money are nice, they aren't going to throw their arms around you and give you a hug.

My mate Vivienne is like so many of us girls. She spent so much of her life worrying about her figure or if she had spots on her face, and was constantly quite negative about herself. Then her best friend Sara, 28, fell ill with cancer.

'It was like, boom! Suddenly everything was put into perspective. I'd taken my health completely for granted before and now, to see my friend suffering chemo and having to go through what she did, it really brought it home to me how very lucky we are if our bodies are healthy. I stopped worrying about all the little things and looked at my body in a totally different way.'

Again, it's not to say that the things we worry about every day aren't important to us, it's just that we should challenge our thinking a bit when we do worry about these things. Ask yourself: 'Is this the worst thing that could happen to me?' If the answer is no, and it probably is, then you can start to focus on the things you can appreciate, or the things you can do to change your life for the better.

Una, 29, was left paralysed after a car accident. To come to terms with her new life in a wheelchair, she told me she had decided to view the world differently.

'When I started to learn to be independent again, I just saw the world with a feeling of "I am the lucky one" as little blessings began to count. Like seeing the sunset or wheeling myself along a beach promenade. I just knew I was lucky to be alive.'

Sometimes it's in tough times like this that we feel the need to grab hold of and cherish the small things. It's these moments of peace and contentment, which we can all experience in everyday life, that can help see us through, no matter the problem. By seeing what we *have* got, rather than what we haven't, we can instantly decide that life isn't as bad as we thought.

'The happiest people don't have the best of everything, they just make the best of everything they have.' Karen S. Magee, motivational author

Instant ways to feel more grateful!

How can you feel grateful for what you have, especially when you're feeling miserable about yourself or your situation in life? In fact, this is exactly the time to take stock of what you feel grateful for. It can help alleviate your painful feelings and put you on a more even keel. Simply listing the things you love can even bring you happiness. Here are a few suggestions for how to go about counting your blessings.

o Keep a 'blessings' journal. Write a list of things in your life you are completely happy about or grateful for. Think of obvious things, such as friends or family, and list things that happened during your day. Maybe someone was kind to you, or you saw something beautiful in nature, or you realised how much you love doing something. Write down the positive things from your day every evening and notice the difference in your thinking when you're not focused on the negative!

- Stick up your blessings around your house! Sounds a bit bonkers, but writing them on Post-it notes and leaving them either for yourself or a loved one can remind you of what's important.

- Share your gratitude. Tell your loved ones you love them, how important they are to you. Sharing your gratitude openly is one way of reinforcing it.

- Write letters to people in your past who have helped you or who were an inspiration, and thank them for what they did, even if it's people you've not spoken to for years. It could be a schoolteacher, a neighbour, a parent, a good friend. Being conscious of how we were influenced or helped, and thanking someone for it, is a very positive thing to do and can help us feel happier – and imagine how happy they'll be to receive it!

Here is a list I wrote at a time when I was struggling to eat, couldn't sleep and was still mourning the loss of my old self:

Things I am grateful for:
1) *People who love me and want me to get better: Mum, Dad, my sister and brother, Mr Jawad, my friends.*
2) *Managing to survive. I can now walk and talk again. Many people in intensive care never get out. I survived!*
3) *I am not completely blind.*

What are *you* grateful for? Can you see how these are great things to celebrate and hold closer to your heart? The things we are grateful for are so often the things we want to live for.

Some points to get you counting your blessings:

o **Focus on what you *have* got, rather than what you *haven't*.** Scientific research has shown that feeling grateful for the good things in our lives also reminds us to take responsibility for protecting them. This lets us live happier and more optimistic lives, confident in the knowledge that these good things are secure and here to stay.

o **Celebrate the good things that happen every day.** Get in the habit of noticing nice things and take the time to acknowledge them. These positives can take you by surprise and have the amazing power to wipe the not-so-nice things from your memory.

o **Remember that things could always be worse.** However bad things are, there's probably still something you wouldn't want to lose or have taken away. Identify what you wouldn't want gone and feel grateful that you still have something you value. Cling to it and don't take it for granted.

o **Express your gratitude.** Write things down, keep a journal and take time to say thanks to others. Putting your gratitude into words will reinforce it, and will help make others feel good too.

o **Say thanks *today*!** Don't leave it too late to start feeling grateful for the good things in your life. If you don't make the most of them now, they might disappear before you even realise they're there. Acknowledge them and feel glad, so that you don't look back with regret.

61

CHAPTER 4

Faith, belief and trust

Faith and hope are the cornerstones of survival. They are what keep pointing us towards a better future and make us feel secure that some power will take over to help us overcome our pain. But how do we find them within ourselves when things seem bleak? Without the faith that one day I'd get through my ordeal, or the belief that things would get better, I don't think I'd have been able to cope. Here, I want to show you how just *believing* that things will get better will help make it come true. We'll also have a look at how trust, faith and belief go hand in hand towards making us stronger.

> **'A faith is a necessity to a man. Woe to him who believes in nothing.'** Victor Hugo

Keeping the faith

You've heard this phrase a thousand times, but what does it really mean? As much as it's important to take responsibility for what we can change, sometimes we can find great solace in taking a step back and simply letting ourselves believe that there can and will be a positive outcome to what we're going through. When you are at rock bottom and don't have a lot of emotional strength to draw upon, faith can be your lifeline to getting better. You don't have to think, you just have to feel. You don't need to go any further than that. It's a powerful mindset that also gives us a hopefulness that can get us through so much in all aspects of our lives.

We experience this feeling more than we even realise – we apply our faith and belief to all kinds of things, even in situations like assuming your train won't be running late when you're already late for work! Take that a step further, and apply that feeling to let yourself simply believe that you *will* get better when you're in a dark place. Hold on to that feeling with everything you've got. Simply having the conviction that someday I would no longer suffer is one of the biggest things that got me through my ordeal.

Pillars of faith

Identifying what you wish to believe in can make you realise what you want more (or less) of in your life.

When I think of the faith within myself, I break it down into a few things:

o I believe in the power of the human spirit, which can overcome all adversities. If something breaks you, it's only because you have allowed it to.

o I've been through the worst and so now I know I can get through anything. There is often something worse that has happened to you. Think about how you got through other bad times – this can help put things into perspective.

It sounds so simple, but faith is a way of handing over some of the burden to the 'forces that be'. You don't need to know how, or actually do anything, you just have to decide this is what you believe will happen. Some people can find faith as simply as that, others find it through religion or meditation, but however you come to it, it will help to carry you more than you can possibly imagine. You can see it in others, especially if they stop believing or stop having hope and faith – they crumble.

There was a moment when I was in hospital just after the attack, when something from somewhere made me believe that I should carry on and keep going. I personally believe it was God speaking to me, though of course I know other people will have their own opinion on that. Whether it was God, a higher being, something deep inside me or an angel, who knows? But I listened, and for the first time tried to have faith that things would not

o Today will be 'yesterday' tomorrow. Have faith that whatever sadness you are holding or experiencing today will be a memory tomorrow. Your current trouble is only a tiny part of the puzzle of your life, especially if you're going to live to a ripe old age.

o My experiences have taught me to see and appreciate the tiny things. Now I try to take a step back if I am angry, frustrated, sad or need cheering up. I look at my immediate environment and ask myself: 'What will cheer me up?' It could be just getting a cup of tea, having a walk, listening to the birds or calling a friend, and I have faith that doing these things will help.

Even if you can't make things better immediately, remember to always 'keep the faith' that things *will* get better!

always be like this and that my health, my life, my mind would get better. After all, they had to. They couldn't get much worse! Something told me to hang on in there, have patience, have hope, and I chose to listen. I needed to listen or I would have gone mad. People sometimes say: 'Ah, but you just thought about God in a desperate time,' but I don't think there is any shame in this. The manner in which you find faith or hope doesn't matter, the fact that it makes you feel stronger is what counts, and faith will always make you feel stronger. If you have belief in a positive outcome, you're halfway towards achieving it.

Letting yourself believe

You don't need to have religious faith to 'believe' (though that may in fact be right for you). You may have heard of the '12-step programme' used by Alcoholics Anonymous and other organisations that help fight addictions. This programme promotes the idea of a 'higher power', which can help guide us in our lives and struggles. However you feel about a higher power, it really can be comforting to allow yourself to feel that you're not alone. Your higher power can be anything: Buddha, Allah, Mohammed, Nature, Fate. Your faith can simply be a faith in those around you, in the people you love.

Some people find giving themselves over to a higher power an uncomfortable idea but they can still choose to believe in the spirit within themselves or the love of others. There is comfort to be had in accepting that we don't have absolute power and control over exactly what happens in our lives. Just surrendering to the world and knowing you just have to make the best of it, whatever happens, is quite liberating!

My family gave me so much strength during my darkest times. And carrying faith in my heart helped me through those times when they weren't physically with me. I also found making up my own prayers so helpful too. I made one up with my nurse during some of my first operations. We would ask God to place his hands on top of the surgeon's hands to ensure the operations were a success. And we would ask Him to give me the strength to get through it. The routine of this prayer, said out loud before every op, was very reassuring. I say this prayer now for burns survivors that I meet through the charity. Little rituals, whatever they are – religious or otherwise – can unburden us of so much fear and worry.

Faith in yourself

Above all else, the most important thing to have faith in is *yourself*. It hasn't always been easy, but I try to believe in my own power, my own strength, and to have confidence that I will find it when times are tough. Say to yourself that you can do anything – because you *can*. Carry this in your heart.

In those low, dark moments, or even just after a bad day, you can then draw on the strengths and reserves of your inner faith. Knowing that they are there is so powerful. Knowing that you've got through other tough times will help you through the one you're currently in. If a relationship does break up, or you get fired or you crash your car, or whatever happens, you can take a deep breath and then think: 'That's awful, but I am okay and will get through this.' This is a truly great gift. It means that you *know* you're going to be able to provide comfort for yourself. Even if you need to cry and get upset, you'll be able to see light at the end of the tunnel. You can trust yourself to reach out for help. You can be kind to yourself and boost yourself with positive self-talk. You can look after yourself properly: eating well, exercising and not taking unnecessary risks with your health. All this because you believe and have faith in yourself.

Faith in ourselves can also come from observing what other people have gone through and overcome. Or by looking to people who have done great things for others – this can restore our faith that people are good, and in turn can remind us that we too have this quality within ourselves.

The gift of words

The words of others and their faith and belief in you can go a long, long way to restoring your own faith, as I found out when my brother Paul gave this letter to me just before I faced my attackers in the courtroom. In the letter was also a little carved angel. I re-read the letter several times to give me strength. Reading my brother's words made me feel more powerful. Less alone. I knew he was behind me.

Dear Katie,

I wanted to get you something that you could have with you while you were in court, and I found this handmade Guardian Angel. Just go into the court believing in yourself and be confident that whatever questions come your way, or however tough it gets you'll know what to say and how to act. You are the Taboo champion after all!! There was a time when you felt he [Danny] had power over you and you felt vulnerable. That time is long gone. Now he is the vulnerable one, so remember that. You are sitting in the position of power. Each night he is sent back to a prison cell and his life is dictated to him. You have free will and go back to a hotel room with your family around you who love you.

Although I, and the rest of the family, cannot be there with you during the days in court you know that we're all thinking of you every minute of the day and sending our love and strength. Hopefully the angel will pass it on and you'll feel it through her.'

Lots of love, your big bro Paul

His words were a gift and meant so much to me. I know he believed that they would. And his trust and confidence in the power of good overcoming evil helped to give me the strength to get through the trial and believe that everything would turn out as I was hoping. His faith gave me faith. When my attackers were finally convicted, it also helped me to begin to restore my sense of faith in the world.

Trust

One of the biggest things that enables us to have faith (in ourselves, in others, in situations) is trust. To me, trust means having confidence that others have your best interests at heart. So sometimes when our trust is broken we can feel as if we've lost faith too.

Lynsey, 32, was devastated when she found her husband of four years having an affair with one of her friends:

'It was the abused trust and betrayal from both of them which hurt the most. It was deeply wounding and took me longer to get over than the sex itself. The lies and deceit on a day-to-day basis were very hard to recover from.'

Poor Lynsey suffered a terrible betrayal. Trust grows over time, and if trust is broken, sometimes it can never be recovered. But just because someone lets you down once, it doesn't mean all people will let you down, or that the same things will go wrong again, or that you can't ever trust again. It would've been very easy for me to say I would never trust another man after my rape and attack. But in order to have faith when I was ill I had to accept and trust those around me. Like Mr Jawad, for example. If I had refused his help simply because he is a man, I would not be where I am today. I now have absolute faith and trust in him and his abilities as a surgeon and indeed as a friend and supporter of my charity.

Of course, by trusting we open our hearts once more to the possibility of being hurt. We have to be willing to take that risk. It's all too easy to say: 'I'll never trust again,' but it only closes our hearts and minds and can lead to wallowing, bitterness, depression and isolation.

I got a letter from a young woman named Eliza who said she'd had to learn to trust others when she joined a support group for over-eaters. Before this, she had never believed anyone could really help her, but she found herself in a desperate place and finally reached out.

'I went from being a fat teenager to being a fat adult and although I hated my body size it felt like there was nothing whatsoever I could do about it. I was trapped in this cycle of self-loathing and over-eating. But then I was told about this group. It was the hardest thing in the world for me to get the courage to go into that room, a church hall, one cold evening. But I sat down and listened to others pour out their stories of struggles with food.

'At first it felt totally weird to me. Why would I trust a group
of strangers with my problem? But I knew these groups do help
so I tried not to overanalyse it and just had faith and went with
it, and they repaid my trust tenfold. I stopped feeling alone, I
had others to talk to about my issues, and at last I started to
believe I could beat my addiction to food.'

Hannah, 34, also wrote to me about how she found trust in her
own inner strength and a resolve she never knew she was capable
of during painfully difficult times when her beloved mum was
diagnosed with cancer.

'I was so upset when she got ill, as Mum meant the world to
me. During her illness I had to be so strong and learn to trust
myself and my ability to get both her and myself through it all.
Going with her to hospital appointments was heartbreaking.
Mum had always been the strong one but then suddenly I had
to be. Even as an adult, I was still her little girl, in need of
help, but now I realised how much strength I had to give her.
I discovered within myself an ability to cope that I never knew
I had. I found an inner faith and things which had scared me
before no longer do. I feel like it has put things into perspective
and given me a sense of compassion and reliance on myself that
I didn't have before. I can trust my own judgements, my own
instincts more, and I draw such strength from that.'

Trust your instincts: listen to your gut

We all have gut feelings, when the pit of our stomach tells us
something is right or wrong, good or bad for us. It's not our
head or our heart speaking, it's just a sense that hits us as if it's

someone else telling us what to do. Very often our gut feelings are right. You've probably heard yourself saying, 'I knew I should have done that!' There is something very powerful about knowing your own mind and trusting your instincts. Many successful professionals don't just put good decisions down to experience or science, many believe in their instincts as well, though our instinct often improves with our life experience.

Gut feelings tell us when we're comfortable and when we feel something is right or wrong. This is not foolproof by any means, but it's a good place to start when we are trying to find our way through what is sometimes a complex and puzzling world.

Liz, a domestic violence survivor, told me she wished she'd trusted her gut instinct on the very first date she had with the man who became her husband, who ended up using her as a punch bag.

'Right from the start, he was rude to the waiter, and he was quite critical of his mother and sister. There were so many red flags when I think about it but I just tried to tell myself he was just "misunderstood" and needed someone to love him. If I was being really honest deep down I suspected he was just a nasty piece of work. And he was.'

Your instincts might not always be this clear or definite, but sometimes when you have a funny feeling about someone or a situation, try to look into it a little deeper, and allow yourself to trust both the good and the cautious feelings. The chances are there is something in it. We're not always very good at acting on our instincts for fear that we are wrong, but one way of testing our instincts is not to rush too quickly into making a decision that goes against them. For example, perhaps if Liz had taken a little more time to get to know her husband before she agreed to marry him, she may have had her feelings confirmed sooner about whether he was a 'nasty piece of work'. Then she would have been better informed and may have made a different choice in her life. True, sometimes we still make those bad decisions, but allowing ourselves time when we can will often give us the best chance to make the right decision. Other times, we may need to make urgent decisions, and this is a good moment to really listen to what your gut is saying. It may keep you safe from a dangerous situation. Or, it might tell you to leap to a healthy and positive opportunity, like moving to a new place or switching careers to something you love.

Remember that wary instincts are different to paranoia (feeling like the world is out to get you) or phobias (those unhealthy, irrational fears). When you're questioning your actions, take a moment to think about whether your fear is logical; like if you feel terrified to leave the house and you think it's your instinct, as I did for a while, it's more likely to be an out-of-control fear than a good gut feeling. I had to redefine some of my instincts after my attacks, as I instinctively feared another one or that I would be burned again – even by a cup of tea. It was an understandable fear, but not a logical one. The chances were stacked high against anything like that happening again to me. I was so traumatised that I had to overcome those fears with professional help and re-learn what was a gut feeling and what was a phobia. I'll talk more about how to deal with phobias in Chapter 6.

Similarly with paranoia – if you've been cheated on in the past, you may feel that all men will cheat on you and your brain may start to tell you that bad things are happening with new partners when they are actually completely innocent. You may accuse someone unjustly of betraying you just because you've been hurt before, so it's very important to learn the difference between a real gut feeling and a gnawing fear that turns into paranoia, and learn to trust that gut instinct. Again, this is the time to listen to your logical brain too and take the time to calm yourself down and look at the facts. He may really just have been down at the pub with his mates! His phone battery may really have died! He may be giving you flowers because he really loves you, not because he's hiding something!

Even if you've made bad judgements in the past and perhaps put your trust in people who betrayed or hurt you, you can learn from this and move forward more confidently. If what happened to you was so terribly unlucky that you now feel a lack of trust in everything and everyone, it's vitally important that you learn to trust again, but in the right way and in the right people. If you don't let yourself learn to trust again, you run the risk of feeling isolated from the world and unable to build yourself a better life. Go back to the difference between survivors and victims: survivors learn positive lessons from their past or from their pain in order to make their future better, and they allow others to help them get there.

Once I had grown in strength by trusting my own instincts and knowing I could trust the people around me, this helped me to trust myself to start taking responsibility for the rest of my recovery, and that felt wonderful too.

Knowing and trusting your values in life

When we're in a difficult emotional place, knowing what we believe in helps us to understand and stay focused on what we want in our lives. Our personal beliefs are based on the values we hold dear as an individual. Things like generosity, faithfulness, compassion and courage are all values that we may cherish in ourselves and others. These values come from our background, our family, what we were taught was right or wrong as children and how we've developed into an individual as we've grown. Sometimes our belief system might need re-shaping as we grow older and gain experience, both good and bad. But getting to know our values, learning what they are – and what we'd like them to be – is a good way of getting to know ourselves and what will make us happy deep down. This makes the whole prospect of trusting ourselves and our judgements easier.

Identifying your belief system will give you a sense of what's in your heart. If you aren't completely happy with what you find, then change it for the better! It's not set in stone. I was pleasantly surprised to find that my own belief system was flexible and open to change. There was a time when some of the things I valued most were beauty, success and fame. If someone had told me when I was a blonde model that one day I'd be running a charity dealing with burns survivors and helping people to cope with their deepest emotions, I'd have thought they'd gone mad. I simply wouldn't have thought back then that I was capable of it! But as life progresses we can begin to believe in different things and may find that we want a different outcome in our lives.

If you aren't in touch with who you are inside you may find it hard to trust your decisions and have trouble judging what's best for you. And you're likely not to put yourself into situations that will make you feel fulfilled. So take a moment to sit down and work out your own personal belief system. It can reinforce your sense of who you are and ultimately help you realise what you want out of life.

For example, my basic beliefs are:

1) **Treat other people as you would like to be treated.** Such a basic thing, but a big one. It's a moral compass.

2) **What you put out you will get back.** If you put out positive energy and self-belief, you will get this from others in return.

3) **What will be, will be.** There is a feeling of strength to be found in letting 'stuff' go and not sweating too much about things we can't change.

4) **Treat others with kindness.** This is one of the main characteristics I hope to show in my work and life. Even small acts of kindness can give real joy and shouldn't be dismissed. It all matters.

5) **There is nothing more powerful than a smile.** Everyone – young, old, whoever they are – becomes beautiful when they smile. It lifts the mood of the person doing it and that of everyone around them. Another simple act.

6) **Laughter is the best medicine.** Whatever the moment, injecting a sense of humour is an invaluable way to relieve the pressure. I believe there can never be enough of it.

7) **Do everything in heels!** Not for everyone this belief (!), but I love my heels and nothing will stop me wearing them. Even in some of the worst times, I turned up for hospital

appointments with a drip hanging out of my arm and my mask on, but wearing heels ... just because I could! It gave me more confidence, and God knows I needed that. I say that if something makes you feel more self-assured and empowered, do it and don't hold back!

If you are struggling to find faith and to have the confidence to trust, remember:

o **We all need hope in our lives.** We'd be miserable and desolate without it. Only you know what you're truly hoping for – have faith that it *can* and *will* happen and your heart will feel less heavy.

o **It doesn't matter what you believe in, just believe.** Your faith can take any form, religious or otherwise. Whether you put your faith in a higher power, your family, a support group, the power of love or even fate, the act of believing in something gives you a place to look for strength in troubled times.

o **Having faith in a positive outcome will make it more likely to come true.** If you believe something will happen, you're more likely to see the paths that lead there and make the right choices along the way.

o **Personal mantras or prayers remind you not to give up.** It may not be the words themselves that bring you solace and strength but the routine and familiarity of repeating them.

o **Have faith in yourself and your values.** You wouldn't let a stranger make your decisions for you, so take the time to get to know yourself and what you believe in. If you know who you are, you'll trust yourself to make the right choices and will have the confidence to get through anything.

o **Follow in the faith of others.** If somebody else trusts and believes in you, be ready to do the same for yourself. There must be a good reason why they're taking that leap of faith.

o **Open your heart to trust.** If you don't take the risk, you won't reap the benefits. If you've placed your trust in the wrong places in the past, learn from your mistakes but don't let them cripple you.

CHAPTER 5

Embrace the power of positivity!

People always ask me how I stay so positive, and here I want to help you learn how you can be positive, too! Positive thinking is an active tool we can use to pull ourselves out of the deep. Even if we think we're lying to ourselves at the time, positive thinking eventually sinks in. You also have to learn to turn off the negative noise, and sometimes that means tuning out from the negative people in our lives. Let's all tune in to positive thinking!

The importance of the positive

We all like a good moan sometimes, and when life has been unjust, unfair or generally a bit of a nightmare all round, it can feel almost impossible not to get swept up in negative thinking. The next big step in our recovery is to make a conscious decision to be positive.

Never, ever underestimate the power of positivity. It can bring us so much comfort; it can lighten your day, or even just the thoughts you're having in that instant. It's not about burying your head in the sand or being unrealistically and relentlessly cheerful. It's about looking at any given situation and thinking: 'There's some light in this, now let me point it out.'

There have been many situations in my recovery where I had to dig really deep to find the positive, such as:

o When I had numerous operations on my oesophagus to keep it open. Usually doctors only allow around six operations on it but I had 40 or 50! I had to sign a form to say I understood the risk of my throat tearing, which it actually did. This was a year after the attack so it was a massive blow. But when I was back in intensive care, I kept thinking to myself: 'Thank God I am alive.'

o When people stared at me in the street. I felt like a freak for so long. But then I decided to make it their problem, not mine. I knew I was doing a good job just even trying to live a normal life after what had happened. I could feel proud of myself for enduring the pointing fingers.

o When I was looking for a job after I'd recovered enough at my parents' house, I didn't know what to do! It seemed like everything I was qualified for, like being a beautician, wasn't suitable any more. But I stopped thinking about what I *couldn't* offer and what I *wasn't* good at and instead looked hard for what I could do. That's how I eventually set up my charity.

There's always something positive we can think about or do with our day, however small. Sounds great, right? Well it is, and it's so powerful and anyone can do it, including you, starting today. And here's how you can begin.

Switching off the negative noise and turning up the positive!

What you hear and what you say can really affect how you feel. We all have an internal voice, chatting to us constantly in the background. It's that tiny voice inside that tells us whether we can or cannot do something. Maybe it's critical and tells you: 'I'm not good enough,' or 'People don't like me.' Gosh, I often wish I could turn mine off! Sometimes I find myself thinking: *'Don't be stupid, Katie,'* or *'You're worrying too much,'* or *'You're not doing a good enough job.'* But these days I try to challenge it and change it to say something like: *'You're just fine!' 'You're doing your best,'* or *'You have nothing to worry about.'*

Whatever your internal voice says, if it's unhelpful or critical about who you are, it's time to shut it up. Try to drown it out with positive thoughts – even if you don't quite believe them at the time. I really think that if you keep pretending and putting on a brave face, that braveness will eventually win out and feel real. Of course, you do also need to deal with any issues lurking deep down, so you shouldn't lie to yourself or others about your suffering. But sometimes you just have to fake it to make it.

Trying to determine where your negative voice comes from is one way of defeating it. Is it caused by a parent or partner who is overly critical? Or have you fallen into a habit of gossiping with work colleagues, comparing yourselves or judging others? You may not be able to change others' behaviour, but you can certainly change your own, and your thinking that goes with it. When we pause to think about our inner voice, that's when we can take notice and turn it around!

Think of someone you like, who tends to be happy and positive and inspirational – and think of how this comes across. Is it in the way they speak? Or the positive slant with which they view the world? Try to adopt some of their good habits and good vibes! I had a letter from a woman who approached a change in her life with just this positivity. Rosaline, 34, fell ill with an inflammatory condition affecting her muscles and had to take steroids, which meant she put on two stone in just a few months – quite a lot for her normally small frame.

'I just looked in the mirror and wanted to cry when the weight first started piling on. Then I realised for the first time in my life I had proper boobs and a bit more of a curvy bum! So I bought a few extra clothes that suited me and decided to try and enjoy my new curvy figure.'

Rosaline's attitude towards her new shape was incredibly healthy, and helped her deal with getting through her treatment.

My friend Simon discovered that his new part-time job involved getting up an hour-and-a-half earlier in the mornings. He was really funny about being a grumpy morning person, but even in his grumpiest moment he saw the upside.

'I just hate getting up very early, but this was the closest job to my house. But then on the first morning at 6am, I realised how beautiful the start of a day could be. I was the first up, the birds were singing. Actually I could see the positive side! As long as I had my coffee first.'

Of course, in tragic situations, like when someone dies or is suffering, it can be incredibly challenging to find the positives. In his book *It's Not About the Bike*, the famous cyclist and cancer survivor Lance Armstrong describes how, when he was first diagnosed, another cancer survivor said to him: 'You're one of the lucky guys.' At first Lance didn't agree with him! (Perhaps, at that point, he was still feeling and thinking like a victim!) But later, when he'd won his cancer fight and realised truly how precious life is, Lance looked back and decided that, yes, he *was* a lucky person. His cancer had given him an insight into life that most other people will never get and this gave him the opportunity to take a positive view on his life.

Challenge your negative thoughts

Take a moment to write down all the negative thoughts you've had in the last hour. I challenged my friend Lisa to do this. Here's what she wrote:

My negative thoughts included feeling a bit fat and guilty after eating chocolate, feeling annoyed that nobody had texted me all afternoon, feeling rejected after a friend cancelled our dinner date at the weekend, and catching sight of myself in the mirror and thinking how awfully tired I looked. I'm shocked at just how critical I've been about myself!

If you try this exercise and find yourself quickly recalling loads of negative thoughts and 'faults', next try the opposite exercise and list the positive thoughts you've had in the last hour. You'll probably find that much more difficult! But perhaps you will then see how you focus far too much on your negative points.

Perhaps you could resolve to think more positively about yourself in the future. When the sounds of self-worth are ringing out loud and clear in your head, the negative voices become much less powerful.

Taking on a positive viewpoint isn't as easy as just snapping your fingers, but as your behaviour changes, you will find that so too will your mind. Soon you will feel more content in yourself and you will be spreading your newfound energy and optimism to other people. And when that happens, many people will respond by repaying you with more energy and optimism. How great!

'If you think you can, you can. And if you think you can't, you're right.' Henry Ford

Shield your eyes from negative messages

As with what we hear, what we read can also have a powerful impact on us – even if we don't realise it at the time. A divorced mum, Emma, told me she felt so down about the label of 'single mother'. She said:

'I just felt so negative about being a single mother, it just seemed like I'd failed somehow and I wasn't sure why. I felt like everyone looked down on me and my situation and then I started to feel very sorry for myself indeed. Then, weirdly, I realised the newspaper I tended to read was a right-wing paper and was always bad-mouthing single parents and criticising them! As soon as I noticed, and I can't believe I hadn't before, I stopped buying it! And felt better for making a stand. I realised it was other people's judgements that were clouding my own and making me feel bad about my status in life. I wanted to be a positive role model for my kids and knew I was working hard to bring them up, so I started telling myself this and stopped being so negative.'

I once found myself doing a very similar thing to Emma when I was reading bad things about myself in the press and social media. After my documentary was shown on TV, I was silly enough to do an internet search for reactions to the programme. I discovered critical comments that tore apart my fragile self-esteem. And instead of focusing on the positive ones, I found myself unable to read anything but the negative ones. '*She deserved it for dating a man she met online,*' read one. '*If I was her I'd just kill myself,*' raged another.

With tears in my eyes, I kept reading. I even found myself looking at a racist White Pride website, where they actually had whole forums discussing my case. Even though these sites were quite hard to find, I tracked them down and sat for hours reading the comments. Things like: '*Let's find out where she is and kill her,*' and, '*This is a punishment from God for mixing the races.*' It made me feel sick. And I couldn't forget about them. I went back to the site days later to see if any further negative comments had been posted. I was left reeling by the comments – they'd echo in my head all day. I felt so hurt, upset and scared, but still I couldn't stop myself from reading these things. It was like I was addicted to all the bad, hurtful things.

Then I realised what I was doing. I was the one making myself feel bad. I didn't need to seek out the horrid comments online. After all, the internet is full of unregulated sites for any old nutter to post anything they like. Why should I care what some crazy person on the other side of the world thinks of me? So I made a decision not to be a victim of this, and certainly not to be a spectator.

At this point I also ran an internet search on 'burns survivors' to see if anyone had shared similar experiences to mine and I found a few group support websites. The stories on those forums were heartbreaking. Really sad. Some of the discussions were awful to read. People talked about nothing except how their lives had been destroyed. How they'd lost relationships, jobs, money. How they were never ever going to recover. I realise that for some people these sites must be reassuring and perhaps help them feel less alone, so I'm sure these forums have their place, but for me at that point in my recovery, they represented everything I wanted to get away from.

These poor people no doubt led hard lives and needed to vent their anger, but to me it was all so depressing. Nothing was positive. After visiting the forums for a few weeks looking for something to cling on to, again I made a decision not to return to them. I already knew I faced a struggle to get well – and I didn't know at the time if I'd ever live an independent life again – but reading about negative, defeatist attitudes was never going to help me. What I wanted and needed were inspiring stories about people who had come out the other side, who had made it and survived, even thrived. I had already made a conscious decision not to wallow and fixate on the negatives, so these forums just didn't fit with my goals. It was a visual form of negative noise, and by simply *not looking at them*, I could instantly switch off that negative noise.

We can get addicted to feeding on negative information, like eavesdropping on conversations or hacking into the email account of our partner or ex (we all know someone who's done this!). It's a form of self-punishment and no good can come of it. It only gives others the power to hurt you over and over again and will fill you with feelings of guilt and self-loathing. Switch it all off and leave it off!

I can! I will! Using positive language to make positive changes in your life

The language you use with yourself and others really counts, and not just when you're up against it. It affects us deep down and makes us 'see' life according to how we're talking about it. Even if we don't feel it at first!

Sometimes it helps to pay attention to the way in which people speak – in particular those who you think have a positive mindset and approach. My doctor, Mr Jawad, was always very positive when we spoke about my operations beforehand; he always said: 'We will do this and then try that and if that doesn't work we'll simply try something else.' He always used words like 'can' and 'will'; words that implied we would get the results we hoped for. Everything was positive and hopeful according to him, and it gave me such a massive boost and huge faith in his ability to help me, so I trusted what he was saying. And I decided that I would think using this positive language, too.

I also decided I was going to stop thinking: 'This won't work,' 'I will always be stuck like this,' and, 'I can't bl**dy get through this!' Of course I had a whole host of fears and concerns for my future going on, but when it came to my operations and recovery from them, I took Mr Jawad's lead and copied his language whenever I talked about my situation. Even if you don't feel it inside, just picking up the positivity and practising saying it can help to change your view of life. Athletes often do this before competitions. They give themselves pep talks (or their coaches do) and only allow themselves to talk in positives before they set off. It reinforces a good message to yourself and makes success *much more* likely. How brilliant is that?

You can find people who speak positively in your life everywhere if you look and listen out for them. It could be a teacher who is always upbeat or a good friend. If you are inspired by the way that someone speaks, listen to the language and tone that they use and model your speech on theirs. If hearing them speak makes you feel positive and empowered, decide that from now on *you* are going to be positive too. You can be the one who turns the situations around, who chooses to see the bright, optimistic side rather than the possibility of failure. Why not try it?

Beware of energy vampires!

While you're looking for help and working hard to pull your life together, it's wonderful and important to rely on friends, but there are inevitably some people who are negative. Energy vampires are not the blood-sucking kind, but they *will* suck the life out of you.

Energy vampires are the people who constantly moan about their lives but refuse to do anything about it. They never take full responsibility for their actions and always see the blackest picture. Some go so far as to believe they were born under an unlucky star. And you could be forgiven for thinking they *are* unlucky – but only because they believe it so deeply. Even when something good does happen, they brush it off or refuse to be grateful. They snub the good and feed off the bad. They often lead chaotic lives, hate their jobs or are unhappy in their relationships, but despite this they never take action or make positive changes. You find yourself having the same conversation over and over again with them (hmm, could they be wallowing?) and come away feeling drained, tired and gloomy yourself, however happy your mood was beforehand!

They're not bad people, they simply have their own insecurities or are stuck in their own ruts and take comfort in your being – and staying – in the same place as they are (this is not the same as finding comfort and support in someone who is experiencing a similar thing to you, which is a positive thing to do). Energy vampires don't see themselves with a compassionate eye so it's difficult for them to give anyone else compassion. They are quick to criticise your good progress or ideas and will stand in judgement of you.

Take care not to let these energy vampires pull you down too, or to feed off your problems. When you are in a period of recovery, people who don't make you feel good, who make negative comments and who don't add to your life, should be avoided wherever possible. I don't mean this in a nasty way – as all of us have friends in need, and some people are easier to avoid than others, such as close family members. But when you have committed to making big changes in your life, you need to give yourself every chance to make that happen, and energy vampires will just slow you down. When you're feeling stronger, that's when you can possibly help them, but for now you need to concentrate on your own mental health.

Try to focus on those people who inspire you, who genuinely care for your happiness, who make you feel good about yourself. I love the saying: 'Some people are like drains and others are like radiators.' It's so true! So remember not only to surround yourself with people who radiate warmth and support, but to be a radiator yourself. It means you'll also attract more of those people into your life. Equally, when you're confiding in your friends, be aware of becoming an energy vampire yourself. You can talk, they can listen, they can try and help. But if you find yourself having the same conversation over and over again and you keep hitting a brick wall, maybe it's time to look elsewhere for support, probably from a professional (please see Chapter 14 on getting help), otherwise you run the risk of wearing your friends down and they will feel helpless to really support you.

Also, if you help a friend or they help you, then try to see it as a two-way street. If someone helps you, remember to honour their help by putting in the hard work to get better. And always remember that they were there for you when you were down.

Inspiration is everywhere!

If you're looking for positive influences to bring into your life, there is absolutely no shortage if you simply look around you.

Inspiration can come from people, books, films, activities and all kinds of other places if we look for it. It can come from leaders, innovators, even rule-breakers! Many of the great and good in the world are the ones who've stood up to authorities or regimes, like the Dalai Lama who has been outspoken about the rights of the Tibetan people and who has lived in exile for over 50 years. And you don't just have to look at famous people for inspiration: what about your grandmother who lived through the war or your auntie who survived a bitter divorce, or your sister who always keeps a good sense of humour? Each day we can find one person who inspires us. Even the old lady who lives down the road and always keeps her garden tidy. Open your eyes and you will find them.

At times, we can find inspiration and positivity simply from a stroll on the beach, or a walk in the woods, or anywhere with fresh air, greenery and nature. For centuries, poets and writers have found the natural world a constant source of inspiration. Fresh air and time alone surrounded by such beauty can soothe the soul and clear the cobwebs in your mind. It can even inspire you to write poetry or paint. In our busy lives, we often lose sight of the power of just being outside.

So, it doesn't matter where you get your inspiration, but finding outside sources for inspiration will help feed your mind, your soul and your strength.

Words of inspiration

There are so many valuable self-help books on the market, with advice from experts and life coaches, which can help you view your life from different perspectives and discover new ways to address your emotions. Even just picking up a book of positive affirmations (little sayings like 'When I believe in myself, so do others') can see you through a tough time. And how wonderful it is to let your mind get lost in fiction, to escape into powerful or beautiful stories and characters and absorb the ways in which they lead their lives. There are endless novels that can teach you important lessons about life.

The books you find most helpful aren't always the ones you might expect. My friend Lucy is a single mum of three boys and a self-confessed hater of all things sport-related, but she found herself identifying with Lance Armstrong's book *It's Not About the Bike*, which I mentioned previously. The story centres on Lance's battle with prostate cancer and how he beat it and went on to win the Tour De France, a phenomenal achievement for any athlete, let alone one who battled cancer. Lucy said to me:

'I just couldn't put it down. You can sense Lance's breathless struggle from page one. I've luckily never had cancer, and usually I'm the first to switch cycling or any sport off the TV, but his story was so incredible. For days afterwards I thought about my own life and how I could be more positive and his mentality of fighting the good fight really rubbed off on me. Very unexpected!'

Even when we're not actively looking for inspiration, the remarkable lives of others can challenge us to be better in everything we do.

The Secret

One book in particular that helped me was *The Secret* by Rhonda Byrne. I'd heard about it before the attack and knew that it had helped many people, so I turned to it when I felt I needed guidance. At first, I couldn't read because my eyes were still recovering, so I got an audio tape and listened to it every time I had physiotherapy. The message of the book is all about learning to think positively and how it can have life-changing results. The basic premise is based on the 'law of the universe': that is, if you have positive thoughts and a positive outlook you will attract positivity. And who can argue with that?

The book focuses on the idea that whatever has happened to your body, your mind can beat it, and because of what I was going through, that was an important idea for me to hang on to. The lessons that were especially powerful for me in this book were the ones about making yourself feel better and believing in your own recovery. It says: 'Healing through the mind can work harmoniously with medicine,' and, '"Thinking perfect health" is something anybody can do privately within themselves, no matter what is happening around them.' By listening to these words over and over, I started to believe them, and to live them. I didn't have control over my physical recovery but I *did* have control over the mental side of things and I really did want to win.

I even wrote down my favourite quotes and stuck them up around the house to remind me. Don't underestimate the power of re-reading your favourite bits from books or even memorising them. When low moments strike, you can easily recall the powerful words and hopefully ease your thinking back to the positive.

Films are another perfect source of inspiration. A colleague of mine loves *Gone with the Wind*, especially the character Scarlett O'Hara. She told me, '*Scarlett is a strong woman who really faces life's adversities with such a toughness, I just love it. Every time I watch it I feel like I can take on the world.*'

At the end of this book I've listed some films, books and even music which really helped me get through the tough times, or that keep me motivated and upbeat now.

Embracing the power of positivity: points to remember

o **Every situation has its positives.** If you open your eyes and mind, you will find them.

o **Negative noise will only make you feel bad.** If your internal voice is being critical, turn it off. If other people are bringing you down, tune them out. Turn up the positive voices to drown out the rest!

o **Steer clear of negative messages.** You might think that words can never hurt you, but actually the things you read and the information you're exposed to can have a huge influence on the way you feel. Stick to the stuff that makes you feel good.

o **Positive words work!** Our language and thoughts can be powerful tools, both for ourselves and other people. Use them cleverly and wisely.

o **Inspiration can be found anywhere.** Seek out positive noise, positive words, positive messages and positive people. Be inspired by them to become positive yourself.

CHAPTER 6

Facing your fears and phobias

We all have fears. Even those people you think are the most brave have their own demons to battle. Some fears creep up on us, some are caused by events. Some are rational fears, and some seem to make no sense to us. In this chapter we'll look at the reasoning behind our fears and phobias and how you can challenge them. Because, let's face it, when you can deal with your fears, you're going to be so much stronger in everything else you do. If we let our fears run our lives, we'll never move forward. I had many fears to face in my recovery. Here are some of the things I learned about working through them.

We're all scared of something

There is one thing everyone has in common, one thing that can stop us from going where we want to go and being the person we want to be, and that's big, fat, scary, ugly FEAR. I'm not talking about the kind of healthy fear we feel in dangerous situations (I'm afraid of swimming with sharks, too!), I'm talking about the fears we have inside that become stumbling blocks on the road towards finding the life that makes us happy.

We all fear failure and rejection or hurt and humiliation. It's universal and no one escapes it, even those who've become successful or rich or famous! But facing your fear and learning to overcome it is one of the most powerful things you can do for yourself because it opens up your world. Whatever you fear, by tackling it head-on you give yourself a chance to escape an invisible prison you may have put yourself in.

After my attack, I was terrified of *everything*. From the phone ringing to walking outside, to trying to eat a simple meal, to meeting strangers for the first time – everything made me jump and recoil or panic. It made me a shell of a person, restricting my every move and my whole way of being. If I hadn't learned to deal with my fears, I would still be locked up in my parents' home.

Reactions to our fears can range from worry (an anxious feeling before you have to do something uncomfortable, like go to the doctor) to full-on panic (maybe you have a phobia of spiders or crowds and feel you'd rather die than have to confront them).

Whatever your fears, your reactions to them will be just as tangible. My best friend always hates trying on jeans in department stores as she fears being overweight and not being able to get them on or off again! Even little fears can snowball into bigger fears and cripple someone's life to the point that they never reach their full potential. I knew a girl who feared going to the gym because she hated the sight of herself in her gym kit. Her fears became self-defeating, so in her frustration she just ended up piling on more weight and hating her body. Another woman I know stayed in her unhappy marriage because she'd never finished school and feared she wasn't clever enough to get a job that paid well enough to allow her to be independent. Another man who wrote to me so feared his community's reaction towards him being transgender that he hid in secret, feeling shameful about who he was, until depression made him suicidal.

Our fears entrap us into believing in the negative 'can't do' voices and stop us in our tracks. If we don't recognise our fears and face up to them, they can drain us and prevent us from enjoying life, while also stunting our growth as people and holding us back from making brave decisions that would improve or enrich our lives. And when it comes to decision-making, fear can also cloud our judgement. Ultimately, fear can prevent us from moving forward and can make us very unhappy and regretful.

Sometimes we have to face little fears every day (some of which we manage better than others). At other times we find ourselves confronted with big fears and are forced to face them up close. This might sound terrifying, but it can be an incredible opportunity. This is what happened to Joyce, 50, who told me she was asked to give a speech at her daughter's wedding. She couldn't think of anything worse than standing up in front of a room full of friends and family and having everyone look at her while she read something personal out loud.

'The thought completely panicked me, but I didn't want to admit this to my daughter and I didn't want to let her down. Despite never having spoken in a large group before, I practised in front of the mirror for months beforehand. Then I took some advice on breathing techniques to calm down. Then on the big day I took a gulp of Rescue Remedy [a natural herbal remedy that can help calm you] and went for it! It wasn't perfect but it wasn't bad either, and I was so glad I did it for my daughter and she was beaming with pride afterwards and it made me feel incredibly confident afterwards. Inside I was saying, "I did it!"'

Joyce proves that we can face our fears and overcome them, and when you have done so it makes tackling other fears much easier. She also realised that she was much more critical of herself beforehand than anyone else could possibly be, and that in reality, people focused more on the good feeling about her speech than whether or not every word she said came out exactly right. If she hadn't given herself the chance to face her fears and give it a go, she knows she would have regretted not doing this very important thing for her daughter.

Mary, 29, was always very fearful of showing her body in public, like on a beach or in a swimming pool.

'I was super-critical of myself, especially in a swimming costume. It was so bad that I couldn't bring myself to go to my best friend's hen do at a spa resort. I couldn't bear the thought of baring my body in front of anyone else, especially my spare-tyre tummy. It was such a shame, but my fear of what other people thought took over. I will always wish I could have worked up the nerve to go.'

Mary's story is a good warning to us all that our fears can prevent us doing things that will make us, or other people, happy. I'm sure if she had dug down, she would have been able to see that nobody cared what she looked like, they only cared about sharing a good time with her. If her spare tyre bothered her she could deal with that in other ways later, but by being so trapped by her fear she denied herself a great experience. Sure, she may have felt self-conscious, but it would very likely not have been the humiliating experience she predicted it would be.

Challenging your fears

'Replace the fear of the unknown with curiosity.'
Anon.

The easy way in life would be to just accept our fears and let them take over. But what sort of life would that be? So, how can we start to tackle our fears? When you first think you cannot do something and the fear in you starts to rise, let yourself begin to feel it, then start to challenge whether it's truly something to be afraid of. Working against our fears always feels very uncomfortable at first, but be prepared for this and think to yourself: 'What is the *very worst* that can happen?' It seems obvious, but sometimes the obvious is exactly what you need to hear. This question was something my own therapist kept telling me to ask myself when I faced my first fears of going outdoors. I made a list, and while it was easy to put big terrible things on there (like that I'd be hurt again), really the answer to the question was probably more that people would look at me, and that wasn't going to kill me.

Returning to your positive thinking and giving yourself encouragement can work wonders when you feel the panic rise. One of my mantras was 'I can and will do this'. Yours may be something like: 'Everything will be okay', 'I'm liked by other people', 'I'm good at what I do', 'Nobody can hurt me', etc. These phrases can inspire us to do things for ourselves that no one else can help with.

Remember, too, to listen to your rational head in situations where you think other people are judging you (such as if you're afraid to use public transport or go to a party or join in any fun because you are worried what people will think of you). Always keep this firmly in mind: everyone is usually just worrying about themselves, they are generally not looking at or worrying about you or what you look like. Chances are no-one will ever be studying you with the critical eye you use to study yourself. It doesn't mean there aren't idiots out there who make stupid or hurtful comments, but usually everyone else thinks people who say things like that are idiots too, so know that you're not alone!

Learning instant calming techniques can also help. We so often forget just to 'breathe' in situations that scare us. Just focus on your breath and calm it down by breathing in very deeply and exhaling to the count of ten. It will not only work on a physical level, but if you focus on your breathing it distracts you from what you're in a panic about. It really helps.

And once you're on the other side of what scared you, more than likely you'll wonder why you were ever scared in the first place, and you'll feel a huge boost of self-confidence for having done it. But you really have to make yourself do it the first time. And if I can do it, so can you.

Stretching your comfort zone

If you feel that you can't directly address your greatest fear immediately, take it step by step. First, stretch your comfort zone a little. Imagine you're made of rubber! You'll stretch, but you'll also bounce back from the bad stuff. By challenging our comfort zones and following our passions and dreams, we extend ourselves and our abilities, and each time we go a little further, which makes us feel more confident to confront our bigger fears later. It makes us feel more resilient, more confident and more likely to get what we want out of life!

For example, a young mum, Alice, 23, wrote to me telling me how her boyfriend had left her when their daughter was just a year old. Not only did she have to deal with the heartbreak of the break-up, she also had to cope with the day-to-day tasks of looking after a baby, all by herself. This seemed so overwhelming and bleak at first. She had no job, no house and little money. Everything felt like an enormous hurdle – and indeed it was! But at the time she had little choice, so she stuck with it and soon discovered she could actually handle most things that were thrown at her, even those she had previously thought she wouldn't be able to cope with. Six months later, Alice was living in a new house, had started to decorate it herself and was interviewing for part-time jobs. Bit by bit, she'd stretched herself. She told me:

> *'Before my boyfriend left, I didn't think any of these things were possible. But once he had gone, every little struggle stretched me into a person I never knew I could be. I felt prouder of myself for coping now. Doing it alone seemed a bigger achievement. Life threw me a wild card, but amazingly I have more self-confidence and more pride as a result of it, and am even happier in my new, confident skin!'*

Alice's story warms my heart, as it proves how you can be landed in a really bad situation but still come out of it feeling better and stronger than ever. It even changed her idea of the type of man she was attracted to. Now she likes guys who respect and encourage her dreams rather than feel threatened by them. Her successes made the world seem like a less scary place and made her even more keen to do things independently.

When we have stretched ourselves, it's natural to feel a little 'contraction' too. For example, if you've just stretched yourself to sign up for a new hobby or exercise class you might get home and think: 'Oh no! Why did I do that?' but a little fear after a stretch is normal.

After I'd been discharged from hospital, the first few times Mum suggested I leave the house, I just didn't want to hear it. I hated the idea of stepping outside and was so frightened. Why would I want to put myself through it?

But I had to. If I was going to live an independent life, I'd have to go outside. There simply was no choice and there was no one except for me who could do it. It was the same with going into therapy – only I could sit there and talk, only I could decide what to say. Likewise with healing my scars – it was only me who could wear the protective mask every day for two years.

After a few months at home, Mum took me clothes shopping for the first time since the attack. By then, I'd managed to leave the house a few times, but this was different. I was going to be trying on clothes, in front of a mirror, with a face like mine, in a changing room full of other girls and trendy shop assistants. I worried that people would think: 'Doesn't she realise she needs more than nice clothes to look normal?' My mum and sister Suzy were both there to hold my hand, but even so, I knew that one day I'd have to do it alone. I would have to face these thoughts in my head and the fears of being there without support.

Even when things were very uncomfortable or scary like this, I just had to dig deep and do them. It was the only way things could move forward. I didn't want to sit indoors, scared and bored all the time. I wanted things to happen and the only way they were going to was if I *made* them happen. A mantra popped into my head; I held onto it during those difficult days:

'I am Katie Piper and no one will bring me down again!'

I repeated this to myself whenever I thought about going outside, whenever I was worried that people were staring at me, or when I found myself facing any other fears. It's just a funny, silly little sentence, but it did the trick. Each time I said it, I felt a little more powerful and it made me want to fight a little bit harder. I would sit in my room and say it out loud when things all got a bit too much.

So I started to put my stretchy rubber theory to the test. I went outside, I tested myself, I kept doing a little bit more each day, until one day I was ready to face the clothes shops alone. And that day *was* scary. I was shaking as I said goodbye to Mum. But when I got home, I did quite literally bounce around my bedroom! *'I did it!!'* I wrote in my journal that evening. Just reading those words back to myself was so liberating. Not only did I have a lovely new outfit to feel good about, but I knew that I could visit the shops by myself. It made me long to go and try out other things. And that's what stretching your comfort zone is all about – opening the door a little and giving you the nudge you need to go forward in your life, with confidence.

Ways to stretch your comfort zone

o Identify what you think your limit is, then purposefully stretch a little harder. You don't have to start with big emotional challenges, it could be something tiny like running for an extra five minutes on a treadmill, or saving a few extra pounds every month. The little actions add up.

o Do something out of your comfort zone – just for the hell of it. If you're shy, say 'hello' to five new people today, at bus stops or the grocery store or at work, wherever. If you don't normally buy a newspaper because you think you don't understand current events, buy one and make yourself read it anyway. If you are stuck in a dead-end job because you fear you have no qualifications, take a look at a website that might help you gain new skills, for example **www.learndirect.co.uk** or **www.open.ac.uk**. It just might change your life.

o Sometimes we stick with bad habits because getting rid of them is outside our comfort zone. This is a great thing to stretch and test. If you wish you could kick a bad habit, like caffeine, cigarettes or drinking, begin by trying to give it up just for one day. Who knows, at the end of the first day, you might want to try for a second...? Or actively counteract your habit by taking up more of something good for you like exercise or helping others.

If you can do something on a regular basis which you find challenging or something you never thought you could do, then good for you! The confidence you'll gain will make you feel fantastic and will spill over into other parts of your life.

Panic: when fear gets out of control

When we feel fear our bodies react in a physical way. We feel adrenaline racing around our systems, causing our heart to speed up, our mouth to go dry and even our limbs to shake. These symptoms can be very frightening in themselves and can turn into real panic.

I was at my most scared when I had to face my attackers in the courtroom. I had to watch an identity parade to help convict them and I was so overwhelmingly frightened that I actually lost control of my bowel movements. The fear that gripped my body was that extraordinary and is hard to forget. Of course it was embarrassing, humiliating even, but I just couldn't stop it from happening. I was that scared.

Sometimes, terrible fears are justifiable and we have very good reason to feel afraid, but when fear turns into regular panic it can be overwhelming and debilitating. Usually seeking professional support is the only way to overcome this. We'll get on to that in the chapter about seeking help, on page 227.

When fears become phobias

We all have fears – which may be rational and irrational to a certain degree – but sometimes, if we don't confront them and we allow them to become entrenched, they can become so severe, so crippling that they actually prevent us living normally. This is when a fear begins to control us. At this point a fear has become a phobia, and you will most likely need professional help to overcome it.

Tips for tackling fear in the moment

o **Ask yourself: what is the worst that can happen?** Often things are never that bad, if you really look at the situation.

o **Think ahead to when it will be over.** Tell yourself that in two hours (or whatever the timeframe is) this exam, this speech, this interview will be OVER, and that at the end you will feel relieved and will do something nice for yourself.

o **Breathe!** That is: breathe slowly and deliberately. When we're anxious or in a state all our senses go haywire and our breathing speeds up. Deep breathing helps you take control and can slow your heart rate down, calm you and help you focus. Take a few very deep breaths, hold for five and release for five.

o **Think of fears you had as a child.** Imagine something you once found really scary and then fast forward your life to know you can get over it again.

Not all fears become a phobia, though. If you don't let a fear dominate your daily life and decisions, there's always hope that you will be able to overcome it, however long you have suffered from it. I had a letter once from a lady who'd suffered from a phobia of birds all of her life. Every time she saw them, her mind raced with terrible images of them attacking her. It was debilitating to the point that she wouldn't take her grandchildren to the park or go to the seaside in case she came across pigeons or seagulls. Now in her 50s, the phobia had become even worse, but having been brought up in a family who didn't talk about feelings, she didn't feel comfortable seeking help for it.

I contacted her and explained how a counsellor trained in tackling phobias could really help, and suggested she maybe even try hypnotherapy, and thankfully she took me up on the idea. At last she's working on overcoming her phobia after nearly 40 years of suffering!

What sort of treatment can you get for phobias?

I'll go into more detail about professional help for dealing with your emotions later in the book, but there is a lot of great treatment out there nowadays that helps people to deal specifically with the crippling phobias I mentioned earlier. The most common NHS treatment for phobias is called Cognitive Behavioural Therapy, or CBT (for a specific explanation of CBT, see page 241), which is basically a technique that actually *changes* your behaviour.

Getting treatment for your phobias is so important: without it we can become isolated, both out of fear of facing the things we can't control, and also because people know that many phobias may look odd from the outside and so they hide away out of embarrassment. (There are people who are frightened of things like buttons, amazingly, or even of being touched. They know in one part of their brain that it makes no sense, but there is another part of their brain that is totally convinced that these things may harm them and panic sets in at the mere thought of having to face their phobia.)

Dealing with your phobias is so vital for getting on with your life. Let's say that you have a phobia about spiders. You might say that you will always be fine so long as you never, ever, see another spider. But there can never be any guarantee that you will never, ever, encounter another spider. And because there are no guarantees, you will live with the fear all the time that somewhere, somehow, you're going to suddenly see one, and this fear can take over your life.

Avoiding things can never result in a 'cure'. It doesn't tackle the problem. Instead, with CBT, therapists help people with phobias to gently take a step-by-step approach to conquer their fear. This is sometimes rather grandly called 'Graded Exposure'. It basically means introducing the thing you fear into your life in tiny doses and then gradually facing it a bit more, little by little. So if someone has a deathly fear of spiders, her therapist might begin just by talking about spiders, paying attention to the comfort levels, and then letting the talk about spiders become a bit less emotional. Then the treatment might progress so that the client is encouraged to briefly look at a picture of a spider. The next step might be the viewing of a DVD of 'moving' spiders. And so on.

Therapy does not often turn people who have a phobia of spiders into individuals who love them, but it can certainly help someone to live in the same world as these creepy crawly creatures. And the same treatment can work for any phobia, like fear of flying, fear of strangers, or heights, or certain activities or social situations – you name it.

During therapy, you might also be asked to examine what would be the worst thing that could happen if you were faced with your phobia. A therapist told me about a man she was treating who was very anxious in social situations and who had a crippling fear of posh restaurants and of doing the wrong thing in them. She asked him what would be the worst thing he could imagine. He said: 'Knocking over a glass of red wine on a white tablecloth in a really smart place. I think I would die.'

The therapist worked with him by challenging his thoughts

about how bad things might be if people noticed his nervousness and if he did the wrong thing. Then, one day, she took him to a smart restaurant and persuaded him to knock over a glass of red wine – just like in his phobic nightmares. And what happened? Well, the world didn't end! In fact a waiter immediately rushed to his side, apologised for the mess, cleared it up in moments and gave him another glass of wine. The other diners even smiled at him in understanding, and then just got on with their meals. The thing about phobias is that they are very real to people and can totally dominate their lives, but thankfully they are actually quite easily cured.

Dealing with your fears and phobias: points to remember

o **We're all scared of something.** Fear is normal. But that doesn't mean we should sit back and accept it...!

o **Fears come in all shapes and sizes.** It doesn't make them any less tangible. You should deal with your fear, whatever its scale.

o **Fear will only hold you back.** It tricks us into self-doubt and clouds our judgment. Fear becomes a stumbling block on our path towards happiness and it's up to us to find our way over or around it.

o **All fears can be overcome.** No matter how long you've had it, how deep-rooted it is, or even if you feel like your fears have become part of your identity, there is always scope for change.

o **Making changes in your life is nearly always scary.** But try to stay rational and calm, face your fears little by little and remember that the fear will soon be just a memory.

o **Overcoming fear brings with it a HUGE sense of achievement.** Fear is just temporary, but your pride will be long-lasting. And with each fear you overcome, it gets easier to face the next one.

o **Be careful that your fears don't become phobias.** If you don't confront your fears, they can get out of hand and become phobias. A big trauma can also turn fear into phobia. Real phobias consume your life and typically need professional help.

o **Don't let fear get out of hand.** If you feel overwhelmed, or your fear has become debilitating or unbearable, please seek professional help. Please see page 286 for some resources that might help.

CHAPTER 7

Taking healthy risks

When we are working though events or emotional setbacks in our lives, another key step is to push ourselves to grow, and sometimes this involves taking healthy risks.

I had to take all kinds of risks in my recovery. Even little things like meeting new people seemed risky, but I'm so glad I did, otherwise I wouldn't be where I am today. In this chapter we'll look at the difference between healthy and unhealthy risks and we'll talk about the dreaded question: 'What if?'

Taking risks can help us be who we want to be!

In my eyes, the people who take risks in this world are the ones who are truly free. By risks I don't mean crazy actions, I mean the kind of risks that we need to take to make our dreams come true, like dating after a break-up, or leaving a job you hate, or going back to school to learn something new, or moving to a new place, or travelling on your own – the list is long and full of exciting adventures.

We sometimes avoid risk because we're afraid of failure and the things we can't control, but if you don't take a risk then you can't even begin to succeed. And anyway, there is nothing wrong with failure. Take it from me: you learn far more from failures than you do from successes! Trust me, every single successful person you see will have had to take huge risks at one point, without which they'd never have achieved what they wanted. Look at Alan Sugar, for example. He's a rich, successful, inspirational businessman, but over the years he's had ups and down and problems and failures and money losses to go alongside all his wins and gains. But he just keeps going and doesn't give up and he keeps taking risks. Good, well-informed risks, but risks nonetheless.

If you decide now that you don't want to take any risks, that you want to have no stress and be safe in your comfort zone for the rest of your life, that is perfectly fine and completely your choice, but if you have dreams and goals that you wish you could achieve, know that by playing it too safe you close yourself off to life and all its new experiences and riches. I'm not saying that travelling the world is right for everyone, or that you should leave your perfectly good life behind just for the sake of change. I'm saying that if you are feeling held back in your life for whatever reason, or that you're missing out on something you want to achieve – something healthy that will help you to grow as a person and that will be rewarding and fulfilling – then this is worth paying very close attention to.

One argument people make against risk-taking is that without it you gain more 'security' in your world. But you'll know from your own life or the lives of others that things change all the time in all kinds of directions. Nothing is really secure and there are few guarantees. I don't mean that in a cynical way, it's just the truth (and it's different from expecting the worst). One of my favourite role models is Helen Keller, a deaf and blind woman who overcame all odds to become a famous political activist and author in the 19th century. She said: *'Security is mostly a superstition. It does not exist. Avoiding danger is no safer in the long run than outright exposure. Life is either a daring adventure or nothing.'* Isn't that an inspiring way to look at risk?

Living your life to the full is all about taking risks. We do it sometimes without even realising it, but often when something feels scary or uncomfortable, we're risking *something*, whether it's opening your heart in a relationship (and risking being hurt), taking a career break (and risking not finding another job), or even just dyeing your hair a different colour (and hating it!). But by avoiding all risks, we actually risk not experiencing the wins in life. If we give it a go, we might find new love, or a better job or our perfect hair colour!

People who never take risks are rarely very fulfilled. And if they become parents, this aversion to risks often has a negative impact on their children. One of the biggest risks I've taken was moving out of my parents' house when I finally felt strong enough. I craved independence, but it came at a cost. My old fears of being attacked resurfaced. I had to risk facing them again (and I did). I had to do everything as if for the first time. Even simple things, such as taking the Tube or getting home at night alone – things most people take for granted – were frightening for me. But taking these risks made it possible to pursue my new dreams and my new direction in life. If I hadn't taken risks, I would never have got my life back and I doubt I'd be running my charity now, the thing that means everything to me.

Steering clear of the 'What If?' syndrome – how excuses can sabotage your progress

'Yes, but the problem is,' 'The thing is,' 'So I'd like to, but,' 'What if X happens?'

If you find yourself saying these things and making these kinds of excuses, you may be putting obstacles in front of you that will prevent you taking risks and challenging yourself to do better things without your even realising it. We can all find valid reasons for not doing something, but I'm sure I'm not telling you anything you don't know by saying that usually there is a solution as well. It's like when your friend says, 'I have no time to go to the gym.' Instantly, you can think of obvious times when she could go. So you know it's not really about the thing that's keeping her from going, it's about why she feels a need to make excuses. The excuses make her feel she has permission not to take action because deep down she feels it is out of her comfort zone. Well, you know as well as I do that it's entirely in her power and if she wants it enough, she'll move heaven and earth to make it happen.

One of the saddest people I've met was a woman named Anita. She had always been very small for her age, even into adulthood, and she had been teased for all of her life for being tiny. It got to the point that when she left school she decided not to go to college to study fashion design, even though she had the opportunity to do so and was a very talented seamstress and could make amazing clothes. It was her dream to be a fashion designer, but she thought: 'What if they don't take me seriously? What if they make comments about my height? What if they think I'm a freak?' So instead she took the safe route and ended up working in telephone sales where people wouldn't notice how short she was.

Ten years later it's a job she still does. Her sewing machine is now kept in the loft because it's a painful reminder of what could have been and she feels it's all too late. This is an extreme example, but it shows how being too risk-averse can stagnate people in their lives, causing long-term disappointment and heartache to themselves. It's a shame that Anita feels it's too late, because she could still return to doing something she loves, even if it was on a different scale to her initial dreams.

If you're a sufferer from 'What if?' syndrome, then take a pad and pen and list the things you want to do – your goals and dreams. Then start writing a list of all the potential consequences if you took steps to make these things happen, and then say how bad they'd really be. I find, usually, that the worst that can happen isn't so bad after all, or it's something you can start planning for – like saving money to travel somewhere you've always wanted to go.

When I was first promoting my charity, I worried so much about walking down red carpets for events. It scared the hell out of me. Especially walking alongside all the beautiful models and actresses you find at those sorts of dos. My 'What if?' was that others would say, 'She doesn't belong with people like that,' or that I'd do or say something ridiculous. But after looking at my fears, I decided I wanted to put myself out there for the greater cause, because I loved talking about the work my charity does and the worst thing that could happen would be to fall over, flat on my face! The risks were therefore worth it. After all, if I fell down I could always get up again! The worst that can happen in situations like that is often just something embarrassing or unexpected but, as ever, it's usually highly unlikely.

When we're feeling like we don't want to take a risk, excuses often come from a place of fear or low self-esteem. Sometimes it's just complacency (or laziness!). Some of the things I have found in myself and other people that keep them from taking risks include: fear of rejection, fear of failure, lack of belief in yourself or an inability to let go of an old belief, or a need to 'control' and know everything about a situation. Remember, opportunity doesn't always land on our doorstep. We have to be bold to make things happen for ourselves and put ourselves in the right situation for good things to occur, such as telling your boss your career ambitions.

When you finally do start taking risks, the rewards will be so motivating and will make you hungry for the next challenge. Go on, get out there and live! Take that dance class, go to a restaurant on your own, don't wait for life to happen, *make* it happen!

'Behind every success there is a painful history.'
Anon.

Positive vs. negative risk taking

Positive risks are the ones we take knowing that a good outcome will make us feel fulfilled and better about ourselves. But what about negative risks? We all know reckless, impulsive types: people who go out and get drunk just for the sake of it, who ditch jobs on a whim, or who don't use contraception in casual relationships, or refuse to wear seat belts, or simply take silly unnecessary risks for fun or just because they can, or even because they feel life is boring without these kinds of risks. Unnecessary risks often offer temporary pleasure or a 'high', and can make fools of us all. Impulsive behaviour can be a sign of other underlying issues, such as depression or low self-esteem. Often, our instincts will tell us what's an impulsive risk, so listen to them.

If we're taking risks with our physical or emotional health or taking a risk when we already know the outcome is unlikely to be good, then we're gambling and need to be prepared to lose! People who take reckless risks often do so from a place of anger, or frustration or sadness. They think their 'devil may care' attitude makes them strong but actually they're not thinking through the consequences. They tend to fail or end up hurting themselves. They are often the same people who think: 'Well I tried, but it seems everything is against me,' and then usually blame someone else for their failure.

Faye, 43, knows this too well. She had an affair with a work colleague and paid a heavy price afterwards.

> *'It wasn't even because I didn't love my husband. I was just bored. We'd been married for 15 years, had two kids, things were stale, predictable. Suddenly this man at work was paying me so much attention. I was flattered and felt excited for the first time in years. Even as I made the decision to reciprocate the attention, I knew it was wrong and risky but I justified it by blaming my husband's lack of attention. I even confided in my best friend, who told me not to do it. The risk seemed worth it at the time, but I knew the odds were high. I only slept with this man three times before confessing to my husband over a bottle of wine. He couldn't forgive me and now we're divorcing. A divorce I don't want.'*

Faye paid a heavy price for taking such a risk, but she had it within her not to follow through with it. Her gut told her not to – even her friend advised her not to – and she knew that most affairs end in pain, but for the sake of short-term pleasure she ignored these powerful signals and took the risk anyway. It's good that she accepts full responsibility for her actions, but even though she is finding a way to put her life back together, she wishes she could turn back the clock and have a chance to make a different decision.

Even more mundane risks can have terrible consequences when we know, going in, that we're making a bad decision. Elaine, 23, went on a holiday to Spain with her friends and really wanted to soak up the sun, so she decided to be a bit reckless and go without sunscreen. It seems a small negative risk but she ended up in A & E.

> *'I knew the sensible thing would've been to put on lotion, but I just thought it would stop me from tanning as quickly, so thought I'd just take the risk. By day three of the holiday, I was in agony. My skin was blistered and I had sunstroke! I had to spend a night in hospital and it ruined my holiday. In hindsight I was stupid, I knew what the sensible thing to do was, I just chose to ignore it!'*

The best risks are the ones which we enter into being as informed as possible, knowing as many outcomes, consequences and opportunities as we can, and how to deal with them. We can't control everything, but information is empowering. If you're thinking of changing jobs, try to find out what the turnover of staff is in potential new companies and how contented people are. If you're risking your heart in a relationship, find out a bit about that person's relationship history, meet their friends and make a judgement after properly getting to know them. If you want to take a year off and travel, write up a plan for how you're going to achieve it. If there are any red flags, listen to your gut feelings. Weighing up the pros and cons of a risk is a good start, and deciding what personal sacrifice you need to make in terms of your energy and time is sensible. And it gives the risk you are taking a much better chance of success too!

Now, it's important to know that some impulsive risks are worth taking too, risks that may surprise us and which make us laugh (like if a comedian picks you out of the audience and makes you go on stage, or when you do something like grabbing your partner and dancing in the middle of a park for no reason). Absolutely go for them if they feel right; you'll know which are the safe ones and which are the stupid ones – trust your gut. If they're joyful and harmless, have fun!

Effective risk takers say:
'I've spoken to X and they have done it, and so can I.'
'I know where I am going with this.'
'I've read about it as much as possible.'
'I want to learn more before I make a decision.'
'What are the consequences of not taking the risk?'
'Am I being too impulsive?'
*'I have weighed up the consequences and believe I am prepared to
    handle any outcome.'*

Non-effective risk takers say:
'I've not got a clue but am doing it anyway.'
'Who cares? I am sure it doesn't matter.'
'I know as much as I want to know.'
'I'm just going to do it and think about it later.'
'I want this right now. Who cares what happens?'

Risk taking: *points to remember*

o **Living a full and happy life involves taking risks.** Don't be scared of them, embrace them!

o **Don't wait for life to happen – *make* it happen.** Taking risks can make our dreams come true. It can help you grow and find fulfilment. If you don't take a risk, you can't even begin to succeed.

o **Asking 'What if...?' may be a sign that you're making excuses.** If you can find an obstacle to taking a risk, you can normally also find a solution.

o **What is the worst that could happen?** The answer to this question probably isn't very bad at all, especially if you look at it in the grand scheme of things.

o **Look before you leap.** Go into risks with your eyes fully open and your plans carefully laid. Beware of negative risk-taking – if you've not thought things through properly, or you're already predicting failure, then you're just gambling with your happiness.

o **Risks can be fun!** Know the difference between negative risks and impulsive risks. Impulsive ones are often harmless and have no consequences other than lots of laughter. Be brave, and take them!

CHAPTER 8

Laughing through the pain

I can say, hand on heart, that laughter was one of the biggest things that got me through my recovery. I don't know how I would have coped with some of the terrible things I was going through if there hadn't been some comic relief. It's something that's a real part of my personality and helps me get through all kinds of difficulties, and it can for you, too! Here we'll look at finding your sense of humour, the power of smiling and all the positive benefits of having a laugh.

Laugh loud and often – even when you want to cry

Even in our darkest times, laughter and humour have the power to snap us out of our pain, even if just for a second. It can really take the edge off a painful situation and, without you even realising, it can help you to regroup. Experts claim that just the very act of smiling can lift your mood and give you a sense of control, a feeling of lightness and a mental boost. And let's face it, sometimes we just need a bit of comic relief.

I found it so uplifting when my family and I were able to laugh out loud during very, very bleak times. Not because we didn't acknowledge the pain or the severity of what was happening, but because often if you don't laugh you'll cry, and on many occasions we'd all had enough of tears. Sometimes you just have to laugh at the ridiculousness of a situation. There is no need to make pain your full-time job.

For example, I had problems with my oesophagus because I'd swallowed acid during the attack, so I had to be fed by a tube into my stomach. One day, after yet another operation, I was lying in the hospital bed with terrible pain from trapped wind, caused by the stomach tube. My head had been shaved apart from one tuft of hair that stuck up like a cockatiel's, I was still half-blind and – honestly – I couldn't have felt more unattractive or unhappy. But the pain was all consuming. It was a grim time.

'Mum, help me,' I cried.

Clutching my stomach, I rolled around, doubled over, willing the pain to go. Worried for me, she called for a nurse to help. But only a male nurse was on duty.

'I can get something for that to ease the pain,' he said.

He returned a few moments later and asked me to remove my underwear. I had to have a suppository inserted in my bum. As if the indignity of looking and feeling the way I did wasn't enough, now I had to have something popped up my bottom too! By a man!!

'I used to be a pin up!' I thought, and then a giggle slipped out.

'Mum,' I chuckled. 'This is absolutely ridiculous.'

Finding my giggling contagious, Mum broke out into a laugh too. 'I know, love,' she grinned. 'It's awful for you!'

Suddenly the nurse was chuckling too and we all had a belly laugh. It still hurt like hell, but the laughter sure helped me forget about it for a minute. Just to be able to stand outside a situation, whatever it is, and laugh out loud can be quite empowering!

Another time, I was playing Connect Four with Dad on the ward. Even though my left eye was blind, and everything was out of focus, I agreed to a game, and – ha! – I won!

'I'm half blind and I STILL beat you!' I roared at Dad.

'I know, I know,' he laughed back, his face in his hands from this spectacular defeat.

In fact, Dad made me laugh A LOT. Once was in the early days when I had to wear a flesh-coloured sock like a balaclava over my head and neck to protect the burns – not the most fashionable choice of headwear! Dad always took the mickey: 'Night, night Earthworm Jim,' he said, cheekily, one evening as he went to switch off the light.

I did a double take and smiled despite myself.

'Gee, *thanks*, Dad!' I laughed, as much as my stiff face would allow.

He was being cheeky in his own way, and it takes guts to poke fun at someone in the kind of situation I was in, but because it was my dad and I trusted him, instead of feeling insulted it just made me giggle (I mean, with that thing on my head I *did* look like Earthworm Jim!), and it took the edge off a grim situation. That laugh was exactly what I needed.

Later on, I told Dad I felt like I couldn't be down around him because he was so upbeat. We did silly things or he'd tell a silly joke or make up a stupid story just to make me chuckle. I thought: 'I don't want to be the person who brings everyone down. I have to laugh too.'

Then Dad told me he felt the same. If he was able to make me laugh he'd do just that! He felt like he couldn't cry while I was still trying to smile. It was a two-way thing and it lifted both our spirits. I genuinely didn't realise this at the time. But it can work – you can be the person who lifts the spirits as well as being the one to have them lifted!

Laugh yourself healthy

Norman Cousins was an American magazine editor in the 1960s. When he was diagnosed with cancer, he read up about his condition and decided to test the theory that positivity can help with healing.

He ordered a nurse to bring him his favourite comedy films and to read him funny stories. He found that excessive laughter brought him great relief from pain and that he needed fewer sleeping tablets. After recovering from his illness, he wrote about his experiment in his book, *Anatomy of Illness*. In 1989, the American Medical Association acknowledged that laughter therapy could truly improve the quality of life for the chronically ill. So get laughing!

I even saw humour in things which annoyed me. When I woke up from my coma, Mum turned up one day with some clothes for me. Although my vision was still very foggy, I watched as she pulled out – horror! – a *velour tracksuit*. And, wait for it, some *Velcro trainers*! Despite barely being able to move, breathe or see, I felt my breath catch. What, was I seventy-five years old all of a sudden? I might have nearly died but I still wouldn't be seen dead in such clothing!

'Mum!' I cried, my voice rasping indignantly and pointing at what she'd brought. 'I might not be looking my best but I'm definitely not wearing that!'

She looked at my dad and they both laughed and laughed. Even in the darkest time imaginable we could find humour in my vanity! And that gave us a glimmer of light in the darkness. We couldn't believe the horror of what had happened to me, but we were still laughing. And nothing is more powerful than that.

When I left hospital, the problems with my oesophagus meant that for the first year I could only eat soft foods. One evening, as I was watching TV and slurping on a bowl of custard, all of a sudden I couldn't swallow. Because my oesophagus was scarred in several places, I couldn't get the custard up and it wouldn't go down! I rushed to the sink and was gagging like mad.

'Come up, come up!' I was screaming in my head, unable to speak.

For around 40 minutes I gagged and retched like a mad woman over the sink, willing my food to come up. Finally it did and the relief was immense. I turned to Mum and started giggling instead of crying.

'Blimey, Mum!' I laughed. 'I can't even eat custard!'

Bringing it up had been such a performance, I just thought 'this is crazy.' Yes, looking back it sounds disturbing and awful, which of course it was, but to me, at the time, it was also bonkers. Even a harmless mouthful of custard was a menace!

Another funny incident occurred while I was living in France at the burns rehabilitation centre. I saw an amputee take off his prosthetic leg and pretend to bash someone over the head with it during an argument. At the time I wasn't used to being around people with such profound disabilities and at first I was shocked!

I just wasn't expecting anyone to find their situation normal enough to make light of it. But actually it was funny, simple as that.

'Every time you smile at someone it is an action of love, a gift to that person, a beautiful thing.'
Mother Teresa

Tips to tickle yourself

o Even the simple act of smiling can make you feel better when you're down in the dumps. Laughing is an even better step. Try it now. Just smile to yourself while you're reading this.

o Watch something funny. During my year at home, I watched box-set after box-set of comedy DVDs. I might have been lying on the sofa, barely able to breathe and swallow, but that didn't mean I couldn't find a silly comedian funny. My favourites were Steve Coogan (as Alan Partridge) and Lee Evans. They never failed to make me ache with laughter.

o Try to see the funny side in every situation. Of course, this isn't always possible, and can sometimes be hard. But there's a funny side to most situations if you try to seek it out. Even if you don't find it, it means you're keeping your mind and heart open to it when it finally appears.

o Think of a time when you laughed until you cried. Even if it happened years ago, remember it and hold the feeling. Relive the memory and feel the joy you felt in that moment. It'll remind you what it was like to laugh and will make it easier for you to laugh at the things happening around you now.

Other people have told me about their unexpected 'funny moments', which have got me chuckling as well. Jason, 31, wrote and told me how laughter lifted the mood after his father had died:

'We'd just had to say goodbye to our dad in the hospital after he'd had a sudden heart attack. Mum, my sister and I were totally devastated. It was all such a shock and so unexpected. We couldn't stop crying. Then a coat rack that Mum had been nagging Dad to fix for weeks fell off the wall onto a picture below, which also fell and cracked. It was a photo Mum had always hated but Dad had loved. For some reason we started giggling and then we were all laughing out loud, like he was there with us, making it happen. We talked afterwards about all the silly things Dad did to make us laugh and what a character he was. It cut through the sadness and lightened the mood at a terribly, terribly dark time. My sister said she felt guilty afterwards, but I told her not to. If you cry hard, you deserve to laugh hard, too. And I know Dad would have found it funny.'

This is a perfect example of finding the funny at a horrible time. Sometimes you just need a break from the pain in your life. That can also be a big signal that there will come a time when things get better. If we can laugh at the hardest times, we can genuinely feel that pain can lift. The realisation that there is hope and light after a dark time is even more profound when you can sense the light in the middle of it all!

Judy, 40, told me about when her sister was in hospital having treatment for bowel cancer. The family gathered by her bed most days.

'It was often quite sombre and my sister was in a lot of pain. One day my six-year-old daughter started blowing up a surgical rubber glove she found by the bed and pretended it was a chicken's head. The whole family roared with laughter and afterwards my sister said she had needed fewer painkillers that afternoon.'

I love this story, and if it doesn't prove the healing power of laughter, I don't know what does.

Whatever is happening, never ever be afraid to laugh and smile in the face of it just because you think the situation is too serious. I mean, do try not to laugh at *completely* inappropriate times, though having said that, if something is really funny it's often almost impossible not to crack.

One thing, though, is to be careful not to use humour to mask your pain. Smiling for the sake of others is incredibly noble and can make both you and them feel good, as long as you're not simply hiding all the other stuff that people who love you want to help you through.

Remember these points and laugh through the pain:

o **Even in the depths of despair, it's okay to laugh.** Humour can take the edge off a desperate situation and help people get through it or find the will to hang on.

o **Some of your funniest moments may come at your most horrendous points.** Don't be too afraid or too consumed to see them – they will really help you cope.

o **Pain is not your full-time job.** Don't feel that laughter or smiles are against the rules, or undermine what you're going through. Everyone needs a break, and people won't take your pain any less seriously if they hear you having a laugh.

o **Laughter can bring a glimmer of hope to an otherwise pitch-black place.** It may be the light at the end of the tunnel that begins to guide you out.

o **Smiling is contagious.** Even if you're not smiling on the inside, if others see a smile on your face, it will raise their spirits. Before you know it, it may come back full-circle and really lift *you*, too.

CHAPTER 9

Letting go and allowing yourself to move on

We hear people use the phrase 'let it go' all the time, but it's not always the easiest concept to grasp or thing to do. We hang on to all kinds of memories and emotions, often at the expense of our future. I had to let go of my old life and learn not to mourn for it, else I never would have been able to go forward. In this chapter we'll have a look at why it is so important to let go of the things we can't change, and how to turn that into anticipation and excitement for what lies ahead. Your life is your responsibility – now is the time to embrace it!

Let go of what's keeping you stuck

There are so many things we hang on to emotionally – negative self-image, critical thoughts, feelings for old relationships, the things we regret, anger at past events; the list goes on and on. Learning to let go of your demons will work miracles in helping you move forward past the things that are causing you pain.

This is obviously easier said than done and I won't deny it takes practice, but one of the key points to keep in mind when trying to move on is that all of those things that you're hanging on to are probably things you cannot change – the only thing in life that you can change is *you*. Fixating on things that cannot be changed won't get you anywhere. It doesn't mean forgetting things that happened; it just means having a healthier mindset about those actions or events that we can never undo.

When you're overwhelmed by loss or grief or heartbreak, or feel very angry about something that feels unfair, it can seem unnatural just to let the feelings go. We sometimes want to hold on to them tightly, to try to find explanations, to refuse to forgive, and we stew in our anger and rage in hope that we can magically change what happened. But we can't. And deep down, you know this. It doesn't mean accepting defeat – in fact, if you can do this, you're proving that you are anything but defeated. We need to let go to survive.

Just after my attack, I scribbled this poem on a piece of paper:

I will never understand
I will never know
All I can do now is try to let go
The hurt, anger and pain
At the fact I'll never look the same again.

This was written in so much anger. Anger at the situation I'd be forced into. Anger at the fact my beautiful face had gone. Anger at all the anguish the rape and attack had caused me and my family. I had so many hurdles to get over during the first year of my recovery. I had to work hard to learn to let go of fear, anger and missing the way I looked because it was making me feel quite desperate when I thought about it all. It was hard, but I had to do it because I wanted *so much* to get better.

One of the angry thoughts that I had a hard time letting go of was: 'My attackers are just sitting in prison, probably thinking about when they can get released. While I am stuck out here carrying the can! I don't want to be this person!' It was the fear of being stuck where I was for ever that pushed me on in the end. I didn't want to be the girl they destroyed. I had come so close to death already and I didn't want to live my life as if I *was* a dead person, stuck indoors, scared, bitter, angry at the world. I had to do something, I wanted to move on with my life. Sometimes I'd simply sit in my bedroom and think: 'I wish, *I wish* I could let this go!'

Unbeknown to me, this was the conscious start of doing so. I believe if you consciously make the decision to let go, and take steps towards doing it, the unconscious 'letting go' will happen naturally. If you cling on, you risk falling into 'victim' status and letting your life run you, rather than you running your life, or you will live a life fuelled by anger or desperation, and as long as you do that, you'll never ever move on. Besides, anger can change our personality. It saps our energy, makes us want to lash out, even at people who have nothing to do with your problem. It can burn through your mind, even making you ill in the process. Holding on to anger – even if you think it's protecting you – will do you no good in the long run.

Taking steps towards letting go: putting it all away

This puts into practice that old cliché: 'out of sight, out of mind'. Putting away the things or emotions that are keeping us stuck can be a powerful statement to ourselves and our subconscious. It also works if you are trying to give up something (or someone). If you want to quit smoking, put away all lighters and ashtrays. If you have been left heartbroken by a partner, clear out their belongings and re-arrange the bedroom and living areas. Getting rid of physical objects related to what we have lost (or want to lose) really does help you put your past behind you.

When I got to my parents' house after coming home from hospital, I put away all my old photos into a safe box. I did it in a celebratory way – I looked at them one last time and said: 'Goodbye' to the old Katie. Then I threw away clothes I'd worn at the time, any perfume that reminded me of the old me, and I even stopped listening to music I heard at this time. This may not be right for you, but it was right for me. This was all part of the process of letting go of my old life, and many of the feelings, including anger, that I now associated with it. (I can look at my old photos now because I've put the past behind me in a healthy way.)

Immediately after the attack, I had felt so overwhelmed with what I had to do to recover and the end goal looked so far away that I didn't know where to begin. I knew I wanted to let it all go and move on, but my brain couldn't cope with the sheer volume of what I would have to do to get there. Mr Jawad helped me so much to see that the best way was simply to pare things right down and take things one day at a time. With each little achievement, I felt I had made progress, which encouraged me to reach for the next target. I also concentrated on making sure each goal I set was very specific, which made them easier to focus on. They included:

1) Manage to hold down a meal.
2) Sleep through the night without a nightmare.
3) Don't jump when the phone rings.
4) Look someone in the eye while talking to them and not at the floor.

Even though these goals from my early days may sound tiny now, at the time they seemed like the biggest things in the world, so each one I ticked off my list was a huge breakthrough.

As well as writing down these goals, I also wrote down as many of my feelings as possible. I expressed my anger, confusion and fear about my loss. This made the feelings more manageable and less overwhelming. Then I carried on with my therapy, and kept the faith that *one day* I'd be able just to let go of my fears and anger about all the rotten things that had happened to me.

At first it didn't seem to happen. I still wanted answers, I wanted my attackers to say sorry and I was still hanging on to the fear. I fought small battles every day. I still had to pluck up the courage to go outside and be free, to walk around without fear of attack at every corner.

One of my therapies taught me to think of a relaxed place while I faced these very real fears. So I would walk down the street, and when I could feel the fear rising and the urge to run away start to overwhelm me, I'd envisage an advert I'd seen for fabric conditioner, where everything was white, peaceful, relaxed. 'Think of it! Think of it!' I'd tell myself, imagining the street I was walking down was a paradise of some sort. It was tough, but eventually it worked. I was letting go of the fear, bit by bit.

Slowly, very slowly, little changes started to take place. I was still having nightmares and in my dreams I always had my old face. Then I started appearing in my dreams with my reconstructed face and I just knew my unconscious must be accepting the way I looked and that I was letting go of my old self-image.

Letting go doesn't always happen at once. It's usually a gradual process and can require patience, but the end result is incredible and it will allow you to move on. As a motivator, think of all that extra energy you will gain from not having your mind cluttered with all that stuff ... and breaaaaaaathe.

Seeking answers: sometimes there is no answer!

Life throws up so many questions, and it's human nature to want to find answers and get 'closure' when things end or go wrong; you may feel you can't move on without this. But actually there are sometimes things we'll never be able to explain or understand. In these instances it's more powerful just to walk away and not turn back to analyse.

What do I mean by that? Well, there are so many events and things in this life that we cannot account for. People do strange, bizarre things, and sometimes we're faced with unfortunate bad luck. Nothing is black and white. You can take a little comfort from just knowing this and so let these things go more easily so that you can deal with processing other feelings. If you choose to walk away, it gives you one less painful thing to have to deal with. You prevent yourself feeling bitter or tying yourself up in knots about why someone behaved the way they did. You can use the energy you'd have spent trying to find answers towards moving on and building your new life, towards doing things you want to do, setting goals, and feeling good about yourself.

My attackers never did say sorry, and so this made letting go of what happened a challenge. At first I couldn't understand how they could possibly not be sorry. In the beginning I kept asking the police, 'Have they apologised?' But eventually I realised I was wasting my time trying to figure it out. And I'd also come to the conclusion they hadn't said sorry because they actually weren't sorry. I started to accept there wasn't an explanation. It was something that *couldn't* be rationalised, as lots of things in life can't be. I decided that instead of anger, I'd just feel pity for them, and this helped me to move on in my own life.

Rejection can be particularly hard to let go of. For example, a woman named Karen wrote to me, devastated when her husband left her. Though they'd been together a long time, they'd only been married for three months when one day he abruptly got all his belongings together and left her with just a note: 'I can't do this.'

'I begged him for an explanation on the phone afterwards. I explained to him I couldn't find my own peace and closure unless he gave me this. But he wouldn't talk to me and later just ignored my letters. I found out through a mutual friend that he'd just wanted to move on and that was it.

'I cried and cried that night. Was that all I was worth? I felt like he'd not only left me, but he was making the pain even worse by not explaining, and that seemed like a double betrayal. I ended up looking back over the entire relationship – eight whole years – feeling it was all a lie. He'd told me so many times he loved me, but had he meant any of it?'

Karen never got her explanation. After her divorce, she never saw him again. For several years she tortured herself trying to understand and analyse why this had happened and she could never find any peace. Eventually she sought counselling and to get her feelings down on paper she wrote letters to him, though they were never sent. She had to find her own 'closure' and come up with her own answers, then leave the rest behind, which she eventually did.

It's not always possible to understand other people's behaviour (sometimes, in fact, they can't understand it themselves, in which case you really have no chance!) and even if they do give you the explanation you've been waiting for, it may not satisfy your questions after all. Rather than working yourself up about finding the right answer, which can drive you mad, learn to let it go. It's kinder to yourself just to begin the work of dealing with your own life, and a more effective way of leaving behind the pain. You can't change the person who hurt you, or what they did, so stop torturing yourself!

Also, be careful not to look back at what happened and think: 'It was all a lie.' This is a harsh way of rewriting your history. Yes, sometimes people do lie in relationships, but often they will have loved you when they said they did, but their feelings might simply have changed – as painful as that may be to hear. Even though the end of your relationship may have thrown up some terrible truths, it doesn't stop the relationship from having had meaning in the past.

You are the only one who can stop the torture in your own mind. It might not happen immediately but if you practise every day saying things like, 'I cannot change what happened but I will find a better life,' and push away any questioning thoughts, it will eventually start to work and you'll soon be free to move on.

Boosters to help you 'let go'

o **Live in the present.** Dwelling on the past – on what has been and gone – is a fruitless, painful task. If you don't feel ready to forget completely, allow yourself just 15 minutes a day to think as hard as you want about your problem then spend the rest of the day pushing the thought away. Choose to focus on the now; the past really doesn't exist any more.

o **Repeat to yourself over and over again:** 'I want to let this go,' 'I am letting go.' Every time you exhale, imagine you're breathing out all the black smoke of what's torturing you and that it's floating away. I really believe that when you consciously want something badly it'll happen on a subconscious level, and this trick really helped me banish my bad thoughts.

o **Talk to people,** especially those who have experienced similar things to you. Ask them how they let go and moved on.

o **Get involved.** When you let go of the thoughts that are tormenting you, they will leave a gap – fill it with something you love or with something you've always wanted to do. You'll be amazed at how your mind switches its focus from the past to what you're focusing on now, even if only in short bursts.

What happens if you don't let go?

Past events and painful experiences or memories of loved ones lost are easy and tempting to cling on to. Sometimes we do it subconsciously, and so you might need professional help to get you to shift them, but generally if we don't allow ourselves time to grieve and decide to move on, we can feel trapped in cycles of negativity and upset.

I met a man named Barry who, at 42, found himself with a failed marriage and a failed relationship behind him, and because of this he vowed he was going to remain single for the rest of his life.

'I just couldn't ever do that again,' he said. *'The pain of being dumped almost destroyed me. I am fed up of being kicked in the teeth.'*

Even though on one level Barry longed for a loving relationship, he felt he couldn't trust himself or anyone else enough to take the risk and love again. He ended up having a series of meaningless flings and refusing to commit, not only hurting himself but also those who genuinely cared about him. This was because he'd not dealt with the feelings he had about his divorce. He'd held onto the anger, resentment and humiliation he'd felt after his wife ditched him a few months into their marriage.

In the end he became deeply depressed and so lonely that he contemplated suicide.

'I simply hated myself and felt so worthless and angry all the time. Everything annoyed me; I even ended up with road rage and found myself snapping at strangers. I thought I was protecting myself by just having flings but now I know the reality is that I'm my own worst enemy. I've wasted so much time wallowing in the past, and without even realising it I probably pushed away any real chance at happiness. But even so, I still don't feel I can let myself fall in love again.'

There are loads of reasons why we hang on to anger, but it's important to identify this anger before it resurfaces. You may not even realise you are carrying it around with you until it starts to emerge in different ways. These are the signs:

o Tiredness – having broken sleep and dreams.
o Irritability – becoming easily annoyed at friends, partners, work colleagues.
o Feeling like a fraud when you smile or laugh.
o Feeling bored and frustrated when you do simple tasks.
o Habits such as teeth grinding or nail biting.
o Always seeing the negative in everything or relying only on sarcasm for humour.
o Are others pointing out your behaviour?

All of these behaviours can be signs of depression and anxiety, both of which can be caused by underlying anger, simmering away inside you. Once you've recognised that you may be angry about something, try to find its source. Then you can begin to deal with it.

Regret only regretting!

Sometimes we bring things on ourselves. It happens to all of us. Regretting things we have (or have not) done in our past is something we've all felt but it is yet another thing that keeps us looking backwards and not forwards. Regrets can be so self-punishing and stop us from doing the very things that make us happy. It's human nature to think: 'Oh, why did I do this or that?

Why did I marry that cheat? Not take that college course? Not call my family enough?' You end up beating yourself up and feeling bad about yourself.

I'm sure we could all immediately write long lists of things we regret doing – if we *wanted* to. Some people have asked me: 'Don't you regret ever meeting the guy who did this to you?' Some people even point out that I made a silly mistake, dating a man I'd just met on Facebook. I could regret the fact I ever moved to London in the first place, but even though those feelings of regret do occasionally bubble up, I work really hard not to hang on to that regret now, because if I didn't, I wouldn't be able to move on with my new life.

While with hindsight perhaps I would have done some things differently, I try to be forgiving of myself and remind myself that thousands of women safely meet and date men they've met online. It's not uncommon. I was just incredibly unlucky. I work hard to remember this every time I start to get down on myself. As difficult as it is, I try to view myself with compassion and use hindsight to teach me lessons for the future, rather than simply wishing I could turn back time – because I can't. At the end of the day, *nothing* will change what has happened in the past, so beating yourself up about it is a huge waste of energy.

Feeling hopeless and angry about the choices you have already made and lived through is classic negative thinking. It doesn't mean you have to change your thinking to believe that everything you did was right, but it does mean you have the opportunity to learn lessons from the things you did, so you can make sure you handle things differently in the future.

All of our tough experiences can add up to *something* positive in our lives, even if they don't feel particularly positive at the time. If nothing else, it means we've learned more about ourselves – even if what we've learned is hard to look at to begin with. It gives us the tools to make better decisions in the future and gives us the ability to help others who may be going through what we survived.

It may be unfortunate, but those negative, painful life experiences can often teach us so much more than the feelings we have when everything is going our way. When things are on track (and I hope for everyone that's most of the time) we generally don't need to stop to figure out why, we're just happy going along with it and enjoying our life. So, try to put a healthy spin on your past actions. Think: 'I may have done this, but I learned from my mistake.' You may have done something remorseful – like cheated on your partner – but regrets won't give you the chance to erase your actions. There is one positive action you can take if you have done something that has hurt another person – apologise. Even if you can't explain your actions, do the other person a kindness and acknowledge to them that you take responsibility for what you've done. Then you can start to move on. I can't alter the past, but I can alter how I think about it. I did what I thought was right at the time – even though now I think differently. Time does change us.

These experiences may sting but they will help you grow as a person, feel more compassion for others and will give you the confidence to cope with other tricky times. You'll be able to trust your own resilience – and what a gift that is.

Reframe your regret

This exercise will help you reframe your past experiences, so you can see for yourself how they helped you grow as a person.

o Think of three things you really regret from your past.
o Now list everything each situation has taught you.
o Write down what positive things each situation may have brought into your life (perhaps without you even realising it).

With the positive side effects down on paper and clear to see, I hope you're now ready to throw out these regrets and focus only on putting the lessons you've learned to good use in your future.

Recognise what you can and cannot control in your life

Often we are prevented from moving on because we hang onto thoughts, behaviours or memories for fear of not being in control of a situation. We don't want to be caught out by a situation that hurt us in the past, and sometimes we go into extreme activity, trying to change everything and everyone around us. If we've lost a loved one, we may do everything to keep them alive in our minds at all times because we're terrified of stopping even for a minute in case we forget them. Or, we may try too hard to protect those who are still alive from anything bad happening. When we are in control mode, we also often actively avoid letting anyone else help us deal with what we're going through.

So many self-destructive behaviours are rooted in trying to control what's happening around us. Self-harm, alcohol and drug addictions, eating disorders – these are all too often about control. When it reaches this point, it really is time for professional help. If you're causing real harm to yourself, I urge you to seek help. There is a whole chapter on professional help later in the book, and at the end of the book I've listed all sorts of charities and organisations that may help you.

When you start to accept that there are some things you can control in life and many more things you cannot, you can begin to feel a great sense of liberation! Your mind will start to thank you for giving it a break from the hard work of keeping control over everything.

One of my favourite prayers is the Serenity Prayer – its message is really inspiring:

God grant me the serenity
to accept the things I cannot change;
courage to change the things I can;
and wisdom to know the difference.
   Reinhold Niebuhr

The message is so basic but right on! I always used to question the things I couldn't control. 'What happens if I don't meet anyone?' 'What will I do if my body is affected by all the operations I've had and I die in my 40s?' 'How will I deal with it if I never have kids?' But now, instead of always worrying about things that are out of my control, I try to focus on the things that I *can* do something about and let the rest go.

Gilly, a single mum, wrote to me in complete despair:

'*My life feels over. I had my daughter at 19 and have been stuck living in the same horrible council estate on benefits ever since. I cannot afford to move, have no family nearby and my daughter is three years old now – it's so boring and repetitive, being stuck at home every day. There is no way out, I can't buy a house of my own, and I can't get a job. This isn't what I wanted in my life and I don't see how I can go on like this.*'

I advised Gilly to sit down and think in simple terms: What *could* she change? What would she have to accept and what should she just let go? Dividing up your thoughts focuses the mind on what your options really are!

Gilly had to accept her current housing situation but she discovered that she could go on a waiting list for somewhere new. She'd have to accept not having much family support but she could take charge and join a support group like Surestart or help out in a community activity to make more friends. Although Gilly couldn't create more money for herself immediately, she could look for a course at an adult-learning college where they provide free childcare, which might lead her to more work opportunities. When we look a little deeper at what is, seemingly, a terrible or entrapping situation, we can usually find ways and means for making small changes while we work towards a big one.

'The best day of your life is the one on which you decide your life is your own, no apologies, no excuses, no one to lean on, rely on, or blame. The gift is yours – it is an amazing journey – and you alone are responsible for the quality of it.'
Bob Moawad, author

Taking responsibility: the only person who can change you is YOU

The only person who can make the changes that will allow you to move on is you. We each have to take charge of our own lives. No one else can run them for us. That doesn't mean you have to do it alone, but you do need to be prepared to take control.

Though you may feel as though your world and your thoughts are spinning out of control, when you're able to stop and rationalise things, you'll see that ultimately you are in charge of how you think and getting what you want out of life. However close you are to another human being, no one else knows exactly what's going on inside your head (thank goodness!). The fact that you're in control is not always an obvious thing to accept, especially when outside events appear to conspire against you.

There came a point in my recovery when I'd received and accepted all the help on offer. I knew the medics and my parents could only help me so far. For the journey beyond, the only person who could do the rest was me. And that was a very scary prospect!

We have to be ready to accept total responsibility for our own lives, otherwise we won't stand a chance of moving on and finding happiness and contentment. It doesn't mean we can control all the events that happen to us, and we certainly can't control other people, but we can choose how we respond to these things.

We may hope that others will simply tell us what to do and think, and there are certainly times when we all wish someone else would do the hard work for us.

But if you rely on others all the time, or wait in the hope that someone will come along and rescue you, you won't ever feel free.

And if they didn't show up to help you, what would happen then? This will lead to your losing confidence in your own decision making. Of course, relying on someone for help is different from being emotionally dependent. We all need help from time to time, but what happens after you get the help is down to you.

Breaking bad habits and patterns

Sometimes if we don't take control of a situation we can find ourselves stuck in habits and patterns which are hard to get out of. These can sabotage our good recovery and make it difficult for us to heal our self-esteem and move on. Even simple things like always checking your phone for a text message (and then feeling low if no one has texted you), or always having chocolate after lunch (and then feeling bad about not losing weight) can be destructive in their own way. But sometimes it's a bigger issue that you repeat, like always falling for bad men, or putting yourself in tricky situations or saying things that you know are going to make you feel awful later.

Again, remember: when we are part of the problem we can also be part of the solution! By recognising what our bad pattern is, we can learn to adapt and change it. I recently learned about studies that have shown that if we do something a number of times (around 20 or so) it can be reinforced in our minds as a new habit. Sometimes it only takes minor changes to make new, positive habits. Just walking to the next bus stop to help improve your fitness, for example. Getting into the habit of having a coffee before work, rather than buying one en route, can save you money. It's all too easy to say, 'But that's how I am, I've always done things this way and I can't change,' but are you just using that as an excuse?

Making changes to our negative habits can add up to so much and is a way of moving on. You probably do things now that you don't even realise you are doing! But I bet you feel the effects of them afterwards. Keeping a diary of your actions and thoughts helps you recognise habits and will make it easier for you to get out of a rut. Look at which habits have an end result of making you feel frustrated, anxious or out of control. You might be surprised at the result! If you have trouble figuring out where to start, begin with the feeling you're having just at that moment (like, I feel worthless or I feel frustrated) and then work back to when it was in your day that the feeling started. See if there is anything you did that contributed to it (like obsessively checking your email, or putting somebody down to make yourself feel better, or doing something yet again for another person who never shows their appreciation).

One of my habits was always holding my head down when I met new people, even though I had grown more confident. I had previously struggled to look people in the eye because I didn't want people to stare at me or start asking questions, but eventually I was just doing it out of habit. I didn't even realise I was still doing it, but people who were close to me gently commented on it. Then I thought: sometimes, people look at you even more if you look like you're hiding something. So I started to hold my head up and look them *straight* in the eye. It did feel uncomfortable at first, but the more I did it, the more I realised they just seemed to accept the situation.

Another pattern I found myself in was always explaining my scars in great detail! People would ask and I would go into autopilot, gabbling on, just trying to explain it all away. But it always made me feel uncomfortable. I realised I was giving too much of myself away. So I broke the habit by thinking of something different to tell people. Instead of giving my life history I simply said: 'I was in an accident and it was years ago,' and then changed the subject back to the person I was talking to. And you know, it worked!

Beth, 27, found herself making the same mistakes over and over again with men. She always fell for arrogant types who never called her back or would keep her hanging.

'I always used to tell my friends they were my 'type': tall, dark, handsome and usually with quite an unavailable air about them. It just felt like those were the men I was attracted to and in a way being with men like that became part of my identity!

But because they were so unreliable I'd get so depressed, always checking my phone waiting for a text or call. Always waiting for their next move. It was exhausting. I really needed to break the pattern. So first I put my phone on silent so that I wasn't leaping every second and then I started to question why I was attracted to these types over and over. After a lot of soul-searching I realised they were men like my father – people who were emotionally unavailable. This was a revelation and made me realise I was the one picking these bad guys! I was the one who invited them into my life, it was all down to me.'

A year later, Beth met Andy. He wasn't particularly tall or overly handsome, but it was his personality and care that made her fall in love. He made her laugh and feel special in a way no man ever had. And she's never been happier. She took responsibility for the type of man she was letting into her life instead of just thinking this was just the way things happened and by doing so she was able to let go of her bad relationships in the past and move on to a happier future.

There are so many negative patterns we can find ourselves falling into. You could be obsessed with your weight and always calorie counting, or constantly worrying what other people are thinking of you, or just always looking in a close-up mirror for any signs of spots or wrinkles. If we examine our lives, we may discover many habits and patterns that we might not even realise we have! And some habits can feel like a central part of our identity, so we may be well aware of them, but just not realise that they *are* a bad habit!

But by looking carefully and thinking: 'Why does this particular thought or feeling *not* make me feel good?' and then tracing it back to a pattern we've fallen into, it can go a long way towards making us change those bad habits and finding the things that *do* make us feel good. Let go of these bad habits and you will find yourself in a better place to create new, better habits and move on into a happier phase of your life. At first, when you break out of a habit, it will feel a little uncomfortable, but if you can live with the newness and the unease that goes with it, your new habits will soon become as routine as brushing your teeth.

Common bad patterns people find themselves in

- Always forming relationships with the wrong type of person.
- Sleeping late, not being able to get up.
- Eating or drinking too much and regretting it.
- Always being late.
- Losing your temper or blaming others.
- Being critical.
- Moaning about situations but not doing anything to change them.
- Obsessively checking email or social media sites such as Facebook or Twitter.

Letting go and moving on: points to remember

- **It's liberating to let go of things you can't change.** If you can't do anything about it, what's the point in worrying?

- **Not every question has an answer.** Letting go is about accepting this, instead of fixating on unresolved issues.

- **Move forward just one step at a time.** Letting go of pain and regret is a gradual process that takes practice – anyone can get there, but you must be patient.

- **The magic moment when you actually let go can be natural and unconscious** – but first you have to pave the way and clear anger out of your path.

- **Anger is a personality trait.** Don't let it become one of yours!

- **Know the warning signs:** you might not even be aware of your anger, but look for it at the root of other negative feelings or behaviours.

- **Find your own closure.** Don't seek it from other people – it may not always be forthcoming.

- **Be ready to apologise.** If you've caused someone pain, saying sorry will help you both to move on.

- **Letting go opens up a huge space in our lives for us to develop in a positive way.** Make room to let good things back in!

o **Regrets only make us look backwards;** to recover we must focus on moving forwards. Only glance over your shoulder to learn useful lessons, never to dwell or wallow.

o **Ditch your bad habits.** They will only hold you back. Let them go and allow yourself to move forward with new, better habits.

CHAPTER 10

Forgive and be kind

We all make mistakes. We wouldn't be human if we didn't. We're all too good at beating ourselves up for our errors of judgement or even for things that happen to us that we had no control over. We even punish ourselves for not being 'perfect' when we've not even done anything wrong. But what about showing ourselves a little compassion, or allowing others to show us kindness? In this chapter, we'll look at how we can treat ourselves (and therefore others) with a little more kindness.

Forgiving yourself: when life is tough on you, treat yourself like you would a friend

When you're suffering or coming through a difficult time, it's easy to blame yourself for your problems and beat yourself up for having arrived there in the first place. But being stuck in a cycle where you do nothing but give yourself a hard time for what has passed can do enormous damage to your self-esteem, your relationships and your future decision-making.

For a time I felt terribly guilty for putting my family through the horrors of having to deal with my injuries and forcing them to confront the idea that someone could have done this to a person they love. I felt guilty for Mum giving up her job as a classroom assistant to care for me. I felt guilty for Dad putting his business as a barber aside so he could provide support for me. I felt guilty for my sister. I used to be her big sister – the one who always looked after her – but now she had to look after me.

I also felt dreadful during the trials. My dad and brother had to hear details about my rape. I felt so ashamed. No father wants to know such things.

I also looked back at myself as I had been: the young, carefree, driven, ambitious blonde girl who was always up for a laugh, and I asked myself 'Why?' Why did I answer him the first time he sent me a message on Facebook? Why did I agree to date such a horrible man? Why did I leave my flat on the day of the attack? Why? *WHY??* It was as if just by asking these questions I could turn back the clock and stop it all from happening. Even today, I could still drive myself mad with questions like these, but the truth is: I made those decisions and they were taken with the best intentions at the time. Would I make those same decisions now? No way, but back then I wasn't who I am now. But I also wasn't a bad person.

Sarah, 31, knows what I am talking about. After getting made redundant and struggling to find a new job, she completely blamed herself for making the wrong decisions at work.

'I just thought I could've worked longer hours or been nicer to my boss. It was like an endless list of mistakes I spun through in my head, driving myself crazy. I was so full of regret and hopelessness it felt almost impossible to even try and get another job!'

This kind of damaging self-talk is the recipe for madness, and can prove horribly addictive. And believe me, sometimes the negative thoughts going round and round in my head made me feel close to crazy! Sometimes we just have to accept that we *did* do those things. Maybe we hurt someone else's feelings. Maybe we acted impulsively and it had a bad outcome. Maybe we over-ate when we promised ourselves we wouldn't. We didn't make these mistakes because we are horrible or bad people, we made them because we're human. And once we get as far as realising this, we then need to find a way to forgive ourselves.

Instead of punishing yourself, you need to start making an extra effort to be kind to yourself. You deserve it, even if you really did bring things on yourself, and it will make things better. You will learn nothing by being too hard on yourself. It doesn't mean you won't feel terrible or embarrassed – these are appropriate feelings, but beating yourself up for too long is pointless. Accepting responsibility for your actions, on the other hand, is healthy and allows you to be better prepared for the future. Try to think compassionately about your life from an outsider's viewpoint. You're probably being much tougher on yourself than anyone else could ever be with you.

Think about it – if you had a friend who was deeply upset about something that happened to her, it's pretty likely you wouldn't tell her off and blame her, would you? You'd listen, try to reassure her that things will improve, make her a cup of tea, bring her some chocolate that she likes, treat her well, pamper her and do everything you can to make her feel good again. So why not also do this for ourselves? We can learn to be our own best friends in troubling times – and equally in not so troubling times! Try to look outside yourself and see if you're doing something which is harming you or helping you – what would your best friend say about the way you're acting?

Sliding into a mode of self-pity and endlessly questioning yourself won't do any good in the short or long term. This doesn't mean we shouldn't learn from our mistakes – we do need to process our own role in what happens in our lives and vow to avoid the same patterns of behaviour, but we also need to remember that we're not perfect. And I promise you, *nobody* is perfect!

Tips on forgiving and being kind to yourself

o Allow others to show you compassion. Surround yourself with people in your support network (friends, siblings, parents, or trusted teachers or colleagues, for example) who will be kind to you and who will understand. Their reassurance can give you the push you need towards being kind to yourself.

o Choose to reward yourself with positive and healthy things. In life there are many tempting quick-fixes to ease our suffering, such as drugs, alcohol, gambling, casual sex, overeating, etc. But often these things only lead to continued destructive behaviour. They end up just being distractions, not solutions and we tend to feel much worse afterwards than we did in the first place. Ask yourself: is this being kind? Or is it a harmful short-term release?

o Go on the assumption that you are being too hard and critical on yourself rather than the other way around.

o Remember that forgiving yourself and those around you helps to release pent-up anger and pain. It frees you from negative, energy-destroying emotions.

**'People can be more forgiving than you can
imagine. But you have to forgive yourself.
Let go of what's bitter and move on.'**
  Bill Cosby, *author and activist*

Forgiving others and overcoming past events

Learning to forgive people or situations is an important part of letting go (see Chapter 9), which is an important step towards gaining control of your life and moving on to create a new, happier one. But often this seems so hard to do. You might think: 'Why should I forgive my lousy cheating ex?' or, 'Why should I let the person who hurt me get away with it?' But by forgiving, you can make leaps and bounds in your recovery.

Forgiving is about releasing yourself from the emotions that cause us real pain. Harbouring resentments is terrible for our body and soul. Forgiving is not about letting people get away with the things that may have harmed you, it's about moving on psychologically, rising above your pain and resentment and finding your own inner peace. Forgiving those who have hurt you is a generous act, but in this situation you are doing it for you, not for the person who did the hurting.

Hanging on to anger and refusing to forgive requires energy and emotion that you could better use elsewhere. For example, Becky, 38, was furious with her father for never being there for her. But she realised her anger wasn't hurting him, but instead it was creeping into and destroying her own life.

She said:

'*My dad was a womaniser who liked to drink and never put my mum or me first. He got into loads of debt and we ended up having to move out of the family home I loved when I was a teenager. My relationship with him affected everything in my life and I became bitter towards men. Then I met Stewart and we got married and had kids. But hearing Mum's tales about Dad still brought me down and reignited my anger towards him.*

'*Eventually I started snapping at the children and suffered terrible migraines. Even my relationship with Stewart suffered. But eventually I learned if I was able to forgive Dad for the past, and then just deal with Mum and try and help her cope with him in the present, I didn't feel as angry any more. Once I'd addressed this, my feelings for him stopped setting off a chain of negative reactions. I needed to let it go. Life is a lot calmer these days.*'

As we've seen so many times in this book, hanging on to bitterness and anger will only hurt *you* inside. No one else. So, be kind to yourself, and try to forgive, if not forget.

I admire those who are able to forgive people who committed terrible crimes against them or others. But equally if you're not able to – and some people aren't – you can 'forgive' by degrees, as a way to avoid holding deep bitterness, which will enable you to move on with your life to live it the best way you can. And that's what I choose to do.

Charli, 31, wrote to me after her brother outed her to her family. She was full of resentment for not having control over her situation and was furious she'd not been allowed the opportunity to tell her parents, in her own time, about her own sexuality.

'*I felt betrayed by my brother after I had told him as a teen, in secret, that I was gay. But I didn't want to tell my parents yet because I assumed they'd be upset. In the end they were very supportive. But it took years to forgive my brother, who I presumed had told them in malice.*'

Charli avoided going to family gatherings if her brother was there and felt such a rage against him that she began to cut herself off.

'*He just wasn't sorry and refused to understand my point of view, so how could I forgive him?*'

But even though her brother never said sorry, eventually Charli realised all the upset she was feeling inside was only *her* pain. Her brother actually felt justified. So by continually holding a grudge, she just made herself feel bad and was becoming estranged from other people she loved.

'*Eventually I wrote down all my feelings in a letter to my brother, never sent it and then tried really hard to "let" the feelings go. Then I turned up at my dad's 60th birthday party with my new girlfriend. I chatted to my brother like nothing had happened and to my amazement everyone accepted my new partner. It was like all the clouds had lifted and it was an incredible experience. By forgiving him, I could stop hurting.*'

Charli's story is a great example of how forgiving can even open doors to closer bonds. It frees the person who is hurting from any more pain. I really believe that once we've got rid of the bad energy for old feelings we've had, it creates room for bigger, nicer feelings to come in! Like I said, forgiveness isn't about not holding someone accountable for their actions, it's just about releasing that steel trap you feel snapped shut inside you.

See compassion in the world around you – people can be kinder than you give them credit for

When you are locked in your bubble of pain, it's so easy to look at everyone going about their normal lives and think: 'How can the world just carry on like nothing has happened when I'm hurting this much?' But the truth is you never know what's going on in other people's lives and what big, dark issues they too might be facing behind their happy facades. You cannot know what they are thinking, feeling, worrying about, just from what you see in a brief moment or even what you see of their lives on Facebook. It's completely unproductive to look at other people and feel jealous or resentful, as you never know the full story!

Try to take the compassionate view that we're all on our own journeys and – just like yours – the lives of others are as tough as they are wonderful. (And to take this feeling a step further, it's far more compassionate to be happy for the happiness of others than to resent them for it.) This goes too for the bumbling way in which some people handle us when we're down in the dumps. They may care deeply, but are just pretty awkward about showing it, or simply have never experienced anything like what you're going through and have no idea how to react.

The first time I walked into a beauty department to look at makeup after my attack, I wanted to run away. Just to walk into a shop with the word 'Beauty' hanging above me on a sign, was so hard. The reaction from the sales girls was exactly what I had dreaded. They suddenly looked busy and avoided eye contact. When I did pluck up the courage to try to look at them, they'd serve someone else. I felt like an invisible person – except I was so conspicuous and different that I was anything but invisible. Some customers even wanted to get away from me.

At first I felt angry that they didn't understand me, that they couldn't see the person I was inside. 'Don't you realise how hard it is just for me to walk in here?' I wanted to yell. (Although imagine their reaction if I had done that!) But then it dawned on me that it was just fear and prejudice, caused by the way the world is geared towards people with disfigurement that made it difficult for them to understand or to see beyond my scars. My face made people shudder because they were scared. Not only scared of me, but probably scared they'd do or say the wrong thing. Thinking like this stopped me from feeling bitter.

When people stared at me, I started to try to think compassionately and concluded that generally people aren't mean, they are curious. I reached into my heart and realised that people who may come across as ignorant and say stupid things probably just need help and educating to understand such an extreme situation as mine. In order to try to empathise, I worked to put my own judgements on hold. Or to think that maybe they were staring or awkward simply because I reminded them of someone they know, or maybe I brought back a memory, or hey, they could have just been admiring my hair or dress! I realised I didn't want to judge or presume anything about them any more than I wanted to be judged.

Mabel, 28, learned this the hard way. She told me that after her sister fell ill with leukaemia she was in shock for days and found herself snapping at anyone who appeared cheerful to her while she was going through such a terrible time.

Then she misheard a shop assistant's cheerful request for

change and Mabel lashed out at her. The assistant responded: 'You look like you've lost a pound and found a penny.'

'Well what would you know?' Mabel snapped. 'My sister might be dying.'

After gently asking a few questions the shop assistant told Mabel her granddaughter had a life-threatening illness too and that she knew what worry and pain a loved one's illness can cause. Feeling comforted by the assistant's words and humbled by her own overreaction, Mabel left the shop deciding she needed to take more care with how she reacted – everyone is carrying their own pain.

Compassion from others can lift you high. Pay it back!

When we're caught up and blinded by our troubles, acts of kindness or generosity from other people can really shake us out of it and help us to see past our tears, even if just for a few moments. It doesn't matter whether it's a big thing they do for you, or just a little gesture, when people go out of their way to do something selfless, it can catch you by surprise and remind you that the world contains good things and good people after all.

It's easy to forget that small acts of kindness go such a long way towards making us feel better about ourselves, not to mention how wonderful it is for the other person. Often we might think: 'Well, what difference would it make?' or, 'They probably wouldn't take much notice,' or maybe you think it would be embarrassing for them – or yourself, but actually you'd be surprised.

Recently I was in Sainsbury's and the man in front of me at the till was buying some toilet roll, milk and a frozen pizza. He told the cashier 'I only have £4, so can you tell me when it goes over?' The man faced having to return the pizza and I just thought: 'Oh that's probably for his dinner...' so I offered him the money for it. He refused, but I just insisted. I'd been having a bad day myself and to be honest it really cheered me up being able to help someone! For the price of a pizza, in a funny way, we both had our afternoons made!

Acts of kindness

I asked a few friends what their recent random acts of kindness have been. In some cases they didn't even know what happened after their mini kindnesses, but not knowing the outcome actually lifted their day as well! Some of them included:

o Putting a spare coin into a parking meter which was about to run out.

o Taking some home-baked cakes to the office.

o Leaving a book they'd just finished reading (and loved) on a train seat with a note saying, 'Enjoy this book!'

o Buying a copy of the *Big Issue* from a seller who looked cold, wet and fed up.

o Telling a stranger that her shoes looked great. She said this had 'made her day'.

o Treating a friend to a bar of her favourite chocolate 'just because' and for no other reason!

We live in a society where people walk past others in need all the time. Too often we don't stop to help – whether for fear of rejection or a worry about interfering. Often, it is exactly these little things that you should do for someone, when you know that if you'd asked them they would probably have said 'no thanks' to be polite, even if it'd make their life better!

This even happens with our own friends. When they are in distress or grief, we all too often think things like, 'Oh, she'll call me if she needs me. I don't want to trouble her right now.' But this is *exactly* the time to call your friend. If you were going through something terrible, you'd probably wish the phone would ring with a friendly voice, so take the initiative to do this for the ones you care about who may need you. In fact, they're probably just too shy to ask for help – so many of us are. The worst that could happen is that they don't take you up on your offer for help. They certainly won't be cross with your offering it, and more than likely they'll feel an immense sense of relief that someone cared enough to reach out. So don't think too much about it, just do it.

Thanks to social media making it so easy to communicate via computers we've also stopped talking as much too, I believe, so I think it's harder to pick up those signals when the people around us may be struggling. (How many people you know post unhappy pictures of themselves on Facebook? Everyone always looks like life's a ball!) Picking up the phone and calling somebody means so much more than posting a message or sending a text. Calling someone and asking: 'How are you… really?' sends a much bigger message that you care!

Receiving these sorts of kindnesses can also teach you so much about yourself. It can be easy to believe that you're past help or not worthy of people's time, but if you make the effort to be open and accepting of the gesture, you will probably find yourself lifted by it, and perhaps ready to tackle new challenges and new obstacles with fresh energy and positivity. This is great for your recovery and also a brilliant way to show your thanks to the person trying to help you.

My sister did an absolutely amazing thing for me, something so unexpected and so generous that it took my breath away. When I was given my mask and was just getting used to wearing it, she actually offered to wear another mask if we needed to go out. I laughed and said no (I mean, how strange would we have looked!? Ha, ha!), but I was so incredibly touched. It made me feel yet again like I wasn't alone in facing my troubles. Even though I said no to her offer, I was so grateful and the impact of her compassion had a huge effect on my heart.

My brother also did a wonderfully generous thing for me. He tracked down and wrote to a brave lady named Pam Warren, who was horrifically burned in the fire in the Paddington rail crash in 1999. For two years she'd also had to wear a mask to aid her recovery. Unbelievably, she came to visit me at home to show me how well it had worked. Her skin looked so smooth and lovely. We talked about her life – not only had she become a successful businesswoman now, she'd also found love. Meeting someone who had gone through what I was going through made me feel overwhelmed with emotion and so encouraged that I wouldn't always be in a bad place, that the treatment was worth sticking with, and that my life could be normal again.

'It really does work,' I agreed.

'It's worth it,' she replied.

This was an occasion of double generosity. First from my brother for making this meeting happen and then from Pam for sharing her experiences so openly.

Meeting Pam proved to me how important it is to find fellow survivors of your experience, and how powerful the need to talk and get help is. After meeting her I didn't feel so alone. Having someone who was positive and who empathised with my situation was priceless.

A small act of kindness doesn't have to be expensive or over the top, either. Recently I was in the car with a colleague when a pill I was swallowing got stuck in my throat. 'Are you okay?' my colleague asked, and not wanting to worry her, I said 'yes' and just coughed (as quietly as possible!). Then she stopped for petrol but instead of filling up, ran inside the shop instead. She emerged with a bottle of water so that I could get rid of the pill. I was so touched. It showed she really cared for me and had noticed I was in distress! Taking the initiative is a lovely thing to do sometimes.

You can spread kindness and help others in an organised way, too, if you prefer, perhaps through charity work or by volunteering (we'll look more at volunteering in Chapter 13). You may decide to focus on a charity that helps others who are going through the same things as you, or you may volunteer in a sector that brings you joy (like with animals or community gardening), or you may want to do things like volunteering to read to the elderly because your grandparents were wonderful to you and you want to give back.

Doing these things not only gives you a tremendous sense of purpose and fulfilment when you see how your kind actions change others' lives for the better, but you will also surround yourself with other people who share your values, which is a healthy way of finding other people to trust! Life is so much better when we feel valued, and being kind to people is a guaranteed way of making both you and the person you're helping feel this way. What a gift.

Some points to help you forgive and be kind to yourself:

o **During hard times, treat yourself as you would a friend.** Look after yourself and be kind. Don't beat yourself up for your actions, thoughts or personality – it will only drain you of energy that is better spent on your recovery.

o **You're only human.** Everyone makes mistakes and nobody's perfect. It helps to remember this whenever you start to get cross with yourself.

o **Forgiveness is for *you*.** Putting aside the pain and hurt caused by other people is not to make *them* feel better – it's to make *you* feel better. Forgiveness will bring you inner peace.

o **Having a forgiving eye on the world can make it a better place for you, too.** Remember that people have their own pain and all kinds of reasons for acting as they do. Don't assume they're out to get you.

o **Accepting kindness from other people can open up your world.** It can give you a real boost – especially if they have similar problems to you and can help shed positive light.

CHAPTER 11

Goal setting

When I decided I wanted to get better, the thing that kept me focused was knowing there was an end goal. Mainly, that I wanted to live a 'normal' independent life. But there were many steps I needed to take to get there. In this chapter we'll look at setting achievable goals, how to stay on track, how to deal with disappointment (not everything will go according to plan!) and how to avoid making excuses.

The importance of goals

In order to start pulling ourselves out of an emotional hole, or to change our life in any way, we have to be able to see ahead to where we want to be. Having goals and achieving them can change our entire outlook on life, not to mention how we live our life itself.

We all have big goals in life, like buying a house or getting married or graduating from university, and we will have other personal goals like learning a skill or a sport, or losing weight or just reading a few more books. In fact, all the things we enjoy or take satisfaction in usually have goals at their root in some way or another. Some of our goals will be emotional goals, like finding confidence, controlling anger or treating ourselves with more respect. But if you've ever become good at something or finished some big task, you'll know that you had to break it down into steps to get there. Taking care of your mind is no different. If you want to change something within yourself, you need to keep your eyes on the end goal (like seeing yourself as a more confident person), but you will also need to set yourself smaller goals along the way. It would be too overwhelming to try to tackle everything at once!

Think of it like running the marathon if you've never even put running shoes on. You wouldn't set out to run all 26 miles at once. You'd either find yourself frustrated and defeated for having to stop before the end, or you'd wreck yourself pushing yourself through, and you probably wouldn't do it very well. However, if you decide to run for five minutes the first week, then ten the next, then continue to increase your distance as you feel stronger and stronger, then by the time the day comes to run the marathon you'll be fit and ready to go the whole distance. Each of your improvements will be worthy of celebration as much as your ultimate triumph of having run your race. If you apply this thinking to the things you want in life, you'll understand why losing weight too quickly or marrying someone after the first date usually doesn't work out in the long run! We can't rush the things we want to do well.

It's the same with recovery, whether physical or emotional. Just after the attack, Mr Jawad made me see that I had to take things one day at a time, and he helped me to understand that I had to set myself achievable goals from the very beginning and gradually build up to my end goal. That way every time I achieved one of my little goals I felt I'd made a huge breakthrough.

When we look at it like this, tackling just one step at a time sounds obvious, right? So why do we tend to make it so hard for ourselves to get started on our journey? Why do we sometimes seem so bent on an 'all-or-nothing' mentality? This is usually because the journey itself feels like it's going to be hard work. But again, if you break things down into small achievable chunks, that's as far as you have to go. If you need to lose 30 stone, instead of overwhelming yourself with this huge task, thinking you need to cut yourself off for ever from all the food you enjoy, imagining a life where you're never off the treadmill or only eating lettuce, maybe try a different way for once and think – okay, first I'll cut down on a few things until I've lost half a stone. Then once you've done that, you can address the next half stone. Each time you reach one of your goalposts, you'll have something to celebrate, you'll have done it in a sensible way, and you'll be that much closer to reaching your end goal. And you know, if you only get halfway, then you are still that much better off! So just give yourself a break and take things a little bit at a time. It gives you many more opportunities to celebrate.

Be realistic with yourself too. Sticking with the diet example, if you suddenly decide you're going to quit all sweets and cakes but you know you love them, you're setting yourself up to fail. It's simply an impossible target. If you said instead you were going to eat fewer sweets, or allow them only on weekends, then you're far more likely to succeed. You'll not be punishing yourself to reach your goal, and you'll be giving yourself achievable timeframes to have all those little wins.

Recently my charity helped a 19-year-old girl who had been attacked in a nightclub with a broken glass, leaving her with facial scarring and a terrible fear of leaving the house. This is the letter she sent me:

'Dear Katie,

My doctors have told me I have agoraphobia. It started when I was 17 after I was attacked in a nightclub and had a glass smashed in my face. I was left with lots of scars, but even though the scars have now begun to fade, my fear has grown worse to the point now that I never leave my house. I feel like a prisoner in solitary confinement. Despite my loneliness and boredom I cannot bring myself to take those first few steps, as I feel like I'm going to have a heart attack at the front door! I try and try but I can't seem to make any progress at all. Please help me. Amber.'

One of our counsellors got in touch and helped her start to enjoy her life again by learning to set herself achievable goals. The counsellor showed her how to break down the idea of leaving her house into manageable steps. One day Amber would open her door, the next she would take one step out, and so on, until she finally reached the busy playground at the end of her street.

On the day she was finally able to make it to the playground, which had already taken so much effort, she turned on her heel and ran all the way home. She called the counsellor and told her, 'I don't think I can do this. It's just no good.' Staying at the playground was a terrifying prospect for her. It was a place busy with mums and kids all running around and screaming, and was the sort of situation that terrified her. But once back inside, she felt so bitterly disappointed in herself. She really started to beat herself up, saying, 'Maybe I'll never do this! Maybe it really isn't possible.' Later on, the counsellor gently reinforced how a trip to the playground would prove to her that she was recovering and how much progress she had made. 'Why don't you try again when it's less busy?' she suggested. So Amber waited until midweek, when the playground was calmer and quieter. She forced a smile, put on her best coat, and took those first few steps outside, trying to muster up as much enthusiasm and as brave a face as possible. This time she achieved her goal and walked around the playground. She came home elated.

Setting your goals

When choosing or writing down your dreams and what you want to achieve in your life, pay attention to both your short- and long-term goals, but always try not to be too vague. If I'd written 'feel better' as my goal when I was first in hospital, I'm sure I wouldn't have known what to do first and I might have given up at the first hurdle. Managing to hold down a meal was a much easier and quicker achievement to tick off that first list I made. Imagine how daunting it would be to write 'make lots of money' when you've not even applied for a job or come up with a business idea yet. 'Get married' is another vague one. First we have to decide what we want in a partner, let alone find a partner who deserves us. 'Get famous' is one I hear all the time from teenagers, but if you want to be an actress and dream of being on stage and grabbing an Oscar next year, then you'll probably find yourself quite disappointed. But if you aim to join an amateur dramatics group and decide to go every week and have fun, then maybe you'll be a lot more fulfilled. And if you work hard and are good at it, you can make it your goal to go on to the next level.

Very few people have their dreams just handed to them on a plate. And you know what? Those who did probably don't have the satisfaction that comes from having worked for it. Of course, our dreams are so important in helping us find our way in life, and they're often achievable – but if you make your goals along the way a little more achievable, you'll be a lot less likely to set yourself up for disappointment than if you just rush ahead. There is no problem with aiming high – in fact I encourage it if it's what you want – just take things one step at a time and don't be afraid to work hard for what you want. Once you get there, you can set your sights on the next goal.

Sometimes a simple brainstorm of your dreams and desires can help you focus on your achievable goals. What do you like doing? Is it a hobby like baking or making your own clothes? A particular sport? Do you want to improve a talent you already have or get back to something you loved doing at school? What would you like to see more of in your life? For example, more time with friends, more fun with your children, more exercise on the weekends, more positivity at work? Or maybe it's something you want less of: less angst about relationships? Less obsessing over your emails? Less losing your temper? Once you start to narrow it down, you can make your goals even more specific. 'I will bake a cake this weekend.' 'I will find out who runs the local cricket team.' 'I will take the kids to see a movie of their choice once a month.' If you come up with very specific goals it is much easier to focus on a plan to achieve them.

SMART goals

I was taught this great approach to setting goals by a life coach I know through the charity. She explained to me that it's important to set SMART goals, which stands for:

o **Specific:** Be clear about what your goal is and what it involves.

o **Measureable:** Make sure there's an easy and obvious way to gauge your progress as you work towards your goal – you should be able to look back and see exactly how far you've come.

o **Achievable:** Don't aim for the impossible or the extreme, make sure the goal is something you can realistically accomplish.

o **Relevant:** The goal you choose must matter and have relevance to your life and the way you wish to live it.

o **Time Bound:** Set a time frame within which you hope to achieve the specified goal.

She told me that when clients need to change their lives, they are most likely to have success with their changes if they form goals that fulfil all the SMART points.

I also find it helpful to break things down into specific areas of my life and apply the SMART goals to each of them; for example my career, my relationships, my health, my lifestyle. Different areas need different attention, and it helps me to take charge of my life a bit at a time. By giving myself targets in each of these areas, it gives me more motivation to keep going. If I just looked at trying to change all of my life at once, it would be way too overwhelming!

SMART goals are smart! Make one for yourself and see.

Being flexible in your goals

In the same way that your problems are personal to you, so are your goals and the ways in which you can make changes in your life to achieve them. I accepted my goals in life had changed after I accepted what had happened to me had changed my life. The second that acid hit my face, my dreams of being a model and TV presenter were shattered. I was reduced to a shell of the person I once was and, with the help of my doctors, I had to rebuild my life piece by piece. My goals and plans shifted to surviving the day, and just learning how to live again.

Two years later my goals were very different and much bigger! Now my goals are focused on my charity, my relationships, and putting the past behind me. Back at the start, if I had said: 'My goal is to lead an independent life the minute I'm out of hospital' I would have been completely disappointed in my progress. Why set yourself up to fail? It doesn't mean it wasn't one of my goals, it just means it didn't make sense to make it one of my first.

Of course I had struggles with some of my goals. Things won't always go exactly to plan just because we set achievable goals – we need to be ready to bend at these times so that we can bounce back and keep going. When I first rented an office space for my charity it was in a building with other companies. At first I couldn't face using the shared loo or communal kitchen while wearing my mask. I didn't want the people from the other businesses to stare at me. So I used to go hungry and sit there desperate for the loo! I thought about taking my mask off but I didn't want to compromise my recovery. So even though I was living independently and was running a charity, I had to set a basic goal like 'go to the loo at work today'. It sounds so funny saying it back now! But eventually I had to take a deep breath and tell myself: 'Just do it!'

Another goal I set for myself when I felt ready was to be able to form relationships and start dating again. But of course this was impossible for me until I'd built up my self-esteem and felt more able to trust my instincts. I was stuck for a while in a phase of believing no one would want me. But working on my confidence and self-worth had made me ready to set my goal of getting out there again! (And I did!!)

Now, my ultimate dream is to open a rehab centre in the UK like the one where I stayed in France. It will cost a few million to set up and then will involve substantial long-term running costs. It will be a massive project, but you know, one day I'd like to make it a reality. It's not achievable now, or even next year, but I'd like to work towards it. I recognise this is my dream, though, and something to aim for rather than something I can achieve quickly or easily.

I also dream of having kids of my own in the next few years. That's the next step, I hope. But ultimately that'll have to wait too and I won't beat myself up about it until I get there either, even if it takes a while.

There's no time like the present

Let's face it: life is short really, so if you have a goal there's no time like now to start on your way. We usually make excuses because we're afraid to fail or because we fear the end result won't live up to our expectations and we'll feel worse about ourselves, or we might simply have just become a bit lazy. Of course it's much easier to think: 'I'll do this tomorrow,' isn't it?

It's all too easy to let things go, or put things off. I bet if you thought about a goal you've always wanted to work towards, you could get up and do something about it right this minute – even if it's just looking up local courses online, signing up to a dating agency, finding out where free exercise classes are held, calling your Gran, or making the decision here and now to finally give up smoking and throwing the rest of your cigarettes away.

The mental barriers that keep us from getting started on our goals are there because *we put them there*. If you find yourself saying: 'Yes, but,' or, 'It's not quite the right time,' or, 'I don't have to do this right now,' or, 'I can always do it tomorrow,' then stop. Turn it around. Think: 'Now is the right time to start looking,' and 'I will make the time.' And if when you say 'now', you really mean 'tomorrow', then I'm calling your bluff, okay? DO IT TOMORROW! That is, unless you've found your spark and just did it, today. (And if so – wow, didn't that feel good?)

You may want to pay attention to something I recently learned called 'The 15-minute rule'. This can nip the time-wasting and procrastination in the bud. Get a timer and allow yourself fifteen minutes, without stopping, to do whatever task it is you're trying to achieve. Often you find yourself carrying on for longer once you get into the flow, but thinking, 'I only have to do this for 15 minutes' is a lot less daunting than saying, 'I'm going to get this ALL done now,' when you really feel you don't have the time. But everyone has a spare 15 minutes somewhere. Whether it's time you need to spend looking for a new job, course or whatever, it's a start!

Have 'me' time to reflect

When thinking about your goals and what you really want, a bit of time alone for reflection can inspire you and help you to get things sorted in your head so that you can make a start. It's quite heartening to give yourself the chance to reflect on the basics of who you are; to define what you want out of life and where things have gone right or where you feel they went wrong.

Enjoying your own company can be a goal in itself. With the constant battering of social media and technology (Twitter, Facebook, email, text messages, web forums, television, the internet) sometimes we never have a second to ourselves to just be alone with our thoughts. Enjoying your own company is all about accepting yourself for who you are, and with your mind free from all the clutter of the outside world, you'll be amazed at the things you notice, the time you suddenly have and the creativity you find that you may have thought you'd lost. It all comes back once we give ourselves the room to let it thrive.

My friend Anya found this when she went away for a hiking trip to the Lake District.

> *'I ended up wandering off alone and it was such a beautiful, peaceful place to have a breather and get some head space and perspective. I started thinking about all the cool things I've wanted to do but never got round to doing. I've always been interested in writing. It was on this trip that I decided I was going to join a creative writing course when I got home ... and I did!'*

Time to yourself can be important, as we rarely think of goals clearly while trying to cram everything into our busy lives or if our heads are cluttered with stress and anxiety and the demands of people around us. On the other hand, if you're lonely, maybe your 'me' time is to go and sit somewhere near other people or to take a class. Remember, that a bit of solitude can be good; but loneliness and isolation aren't.

Try to factor your positive thinking into your goal planning, too. It's pretty much impossible to achieve your goals if you're dealing with depression, constant self-criticism or negative thought patterns. They will kill your dreams. If you are doubting yourself on a daily basis and struggling with self-esteem, remember to turn every 'I can't' into something you *can*, or think about inspiring people who made it through adversity to achieve their goals. If you need positive proof that 'I can' makes things happen, then watch just five minutes of the Paralympics.

Motivation: YES YOU CAN!

We all know the incredible effects that great coaches or leaders have on others. They're capable of lighting a big fire under even the most reluctant people and getting them to do things they never thought they could achieve. Some people are brilliant motivators. I'm sure we can all recall a teacher, boss or friend who was able to get our energy levels up or inspire us to do greater things. But while we should always look for people like this to add to our lives, the majority of the time we simply need to give ourselves a little push and get the party started on our own. And funnily enough, once you take the first step, your mind can refocus to make you want to keep on going. (Weirdly, sometimes even if you're doing something you hate, like housework. Ever noticed yourself in an unexpected cleaning frenzy after putting it off for ages?)

'It always seems impossible, until it is done.'
Nelson Mandela

One trick to help us get started on new goals is to think about past successes. I'd be very surprised if everyone didn't have something they'd done in the past that they were pleased with. That occasion may not come to mind quickly if you've had years of self-doubt or negative critical thinking, but even if you have to go way back to something you did in childhood, you can recapture that feeling. It could have been something simple, like successfully planting a tree, cooking something delicious or taking a good photograph. Whatever it was, think about having that feeling again.

Another trick is to avoid distractions and diversions. You might have gone online to find a new college course and ended up getting sucked into Facebook for a couple of hours. I know I'm always tempted to do that! But be a little strict with yourself and do things like turn off your alerts, close your email or switch your phone off if you're trying to get something done.

Always remember, too, to keep the task as simple as possible. Keep the basics in mind and forget the detail. So if you want to exercise more, try not to run away with the next million thoughts about what that means, like 'I need to save up, then join a gym, then buy exercise clothes, then go three times a week and start training and take classes, etc, etc.' Just make it simple and do what you can right now. Get outside and go for a run, or find a friend to go for a power walk with, or just play frisbee with your kids. Whatever it is, it doesn't have to be complicated or expensive to begin with and you will have no excuses not to do it straight away.

You will already have found all kinds of things to motivate you in your life (your kids, your family, your satisfaction or dissatisfaction in your job), even if you've not yet taken action on the things you want to change, improve or add in. At first my own motivation came in part from wanting to show my doctor and my parents that I was committed to my recovery and rebuilding my spirit, and I was seriously motivated to not let my attackers beat me.

Another motivating factor is sharing your goals. I talked about mine to friends, family and work colleagues. Not only did I get their valuable tips and opinions, but it also reinforced what I was thinking and made it even more real (and much harder not to follow through on!). You'll be amazed at how effective it is to put your ideas and goals out there. It makes them feel much more concrete. It can also bring help to your door. Sharing my goals about the charity meant more and more people heard about it and wanted to help, like the nice businessman who gave me office space!

Rewards are incredibly motivating. Anyone who has a child certainly knows this! In fact, anyone who ever *was* a child knows this. But it's true, if we set ourselves rewards for our achievements, it gives us something to focus on as a nice way of completing our hard work. Equally, though, we must learn not to do the opposite and punish ourselves if things don't go right. I'll get on to more of that in the next section.

Whenever I reach a goal I always try to treat myself. Even if it's for doing some boring admin, I treat myself to a cup of tea afterwards! Just try to keep your rewards appropriate – if you just lost weight, try not to reward yourself by saying, 'Now I can eat what I want!' I know this sounds completely obvious but we so often do it! You don't want to sabotage your hard work. Make sure your rewards are actually good for you (and no, you can't choose shopping for every reward! Not unless you want to go bankrupt, because I predict you're going to achieve a lot of your goals); try going for a nice walk or talk to your friends on the phone. And you know the best thing? Sometimes our goal *is* our reward. For example, if you are creative and love to paint, then you'll have a beautiful painting when you're done!

In staying motivated, one key factor is to avoid motivation killers – don't get brought down by the negative opinion of others. When people put down your aspirations, don't ask yourself 'Why?', just know they have their own reasons, which could be anything from envy to a bad experience, and instead spend your time getting on with your achievements.

Handling disappointment

It's an inevitable part of life that some time or other, something is going to get in the way of our goals. We experience little frustrations every day, like when we have a hellish commute to work. But when we have a lot of emotions riding on our goals it's all the more important to pay attention to how we handle setbacks.

In my recovery I was always disappointed when things didn't get better as quickly as I hoped. For example, after operations when I got an infection that took time to clear up. Or when I tried to feel more confident about facing the world, but got strange looks or nasty comments from people in shops or on the street. It was a slow process of having to keep trying, keep positive and keep going.

I recently worked up the nerve to join a drama course. It took a lot for me to do this because, like so many other people, new experiences involving new people can be a bit scary at first. But I knuckled down and decided I wanted it enough to push past the fear. But when I started looking, all the courses I found were either too far away, not at times I could attend, too expensive or aimed at a much younger age group. Because of all the effort I'd put into getting as far as deciding I was going to do a drama course at all, I found myself feeling disappointed that none of them were right. It was off-putting, but it made me realise that sometimes it takes time to find what you're looking for and it doesn't always happen immediately, and often you just have to be flexible. In the end I found one that satisfied most, if not all, of the criteria, and I'm loving it! I'm so glad I stuck with it.

I met a woman named Lianne who found she had to be flexible and resilient when she started dating again.

> '*A couple of friends found boyfriends on dating websites and they'd told me how easy and great these websites were. So I signed up, but after around ten dates that turned into nothing I just felt so sad and disappointed that I took my profile down.*'

Lianne became quite downbeat about her experience, but sometimes we just need to be tenacious in our goals – I said to Lianne that just because one dating site hadn't worked it didn't mean she couldn't have success on another! Or maybe her profile was attracting the wrong men and she needed to ask a friend to vet it? Whatever it is, you just need to take a step back and work out what your next move is towards your goal. Even if you have to fix the steps along the way, it doesn't necessarily mean it's the goal that's the problem.

Winston Churchill famously said: '*Success is the ability to go from one failure to another with no loss of enthusiasm.*' What a great thought! You certainly won't reach your goal if you give up at the first hurdle. Being kind to yourself comes into play here. If your friend is trying to achieve something, you keep cheering her on, right? You'd think of other solutions, and you'd tell her: 'Don't give up!', so there's no reason why we can't do this for ourselves. Going back for the next round of a challenge, or even round ten, can be tiring and disheartening, but holding your aim in your mind and keeping it clear where you want your life to head can spur you on. You also need to make sure that you're keeping yourself motivated with other little goals, so that where you might have a setback, somewhere else you'll have a win!

Sometimes our disappointment comes from having unrealistic expectations or because we are perfectionists and our expectations of ourselves (and often others) is simply too high. For example, I had a friend named Felicity who was always incredibly hard on herself, no matter how much she achieved – and she in fact achieved quite a lot. I remember she was terribly disappointed when she achieved a B grade in a college exam instead of an A. Even this very good result, which she'd worked hard for, felt like a failure to her. She stayed fixated on that B despite the fact that she'd passed the course, won a place at uni and had done her very best. Her brain was hard-wired on 'could do better', even when it would mean having superhuman powers to do so, therefore even her wins weren't good enough to her.

As important as my dreams and goals are, I do my best to try and avoid beating myself up about what I cannot achieve – I try to focus instead on the fact that I tried my best. That might sound like something your mum may say and it certainly doesn't mean

I don't feel disappointed when things don't go my way, but I try really hard to always move on from my disappointments, learn from them, and then put them behind me so that I can refocus and go forward. It takes work, but it's necessary work, and it's what helps get me through.

Other times, we can feel disappointed because we feel *over*confident in the outcome of our goals. Pete, 18, told me he had been training for a triathlon but later admitted he wasn't trying as hard as he could've done because he felt cocky that things would be fine on the day.

'I was training every other weekend rather than every weekend. I thought I was fit enough and didn't think twice about being ready. But actually I ended up really struggling to keep up. I felt so disappointed in myself for not putting in the work, but I learned a lesson. I'm training harder now. Next time, if I don't finish well, it won't be because I didn't do my best to prepare!'

Goal setting: points to remember

o **Having goals gives your life focus.** The things you're aiming for can affect the way you choose to live and the decisions you make along the way.

o **Your goals are wrapped up with your dreams.** If you dream about something happening in your life, set yourself goals that will lead you there. Then with each achievement, you'll be taking another step towards making your dreams come true.

o **Break things down into steps.** Lots of small, immediate goals are much less daunting than one huge long-term goal, and each success will take you one step closer to your destination. (Plus lots of goalposts mean lots more reasons to celebrate!)

o **SMART goals are specific, measurable, achievable, relevant and time-bound.** With goals like these, you can map out a clear plan for making them happen, meaning success is much more likely. If your goals are too complicated or unlikely, then you may just be setting yourself up for failure.

o **Start today!** It's all too easy to put things off, but make your goals a priority and get started as soon as you can.

o **Say them out loud.** Discussing your goals with family and friends, people who believe in you, makes them feel more real. Write them down, then write a list of all the positive first steps. Who can help you achieve the goal? Can you ask advice from someone who has already made it to the goalpost? Or is there a charity that could help?

o **Find out what motivates you.** Surround yourself with people who push you, remind yourself of past successes and make sure you get rewards! Give yourself the best possible chance to succeed.

o **Disappointment is a fact of life.** But you can always push through it. Get back on the horse and try again, and success will feel well-earned and well-deserved when it finally comes.

CHAPTER 12

Believe in yourself

When we are feeling strong and confident, it's like all the world is going our way. But how do you hang on to that feeling of strength when times are tough? It has to come from within. I really had to believe in myself when I was in recovery.

Though other people can help make us feel good about ourselves, ultimately it's having belief in yourself that will make you truly happy and that will get you through anything. In this chapter we'll look at how to build your self-esteem, how to follow your heart, and how not to spend all your time pleasing other people!

Good self-esteem and strong self-worth are the foundations of a happy life

We hear the term 'self-esteem', but what is it? Well, it's all about how much we value or rate ourselves. It's certainly not about selfishness and putting ourselves above others. How you think about yourself is ultimately how the world will see you and react towards you, so if you feel as if negative things are happening to you, now's the time to have a look at whether you're putting a negative view of yourself out there in the world.

Good self-esteem is the bedrock of a happy life and will enable you to make good and healthy choices. Of course, with all the things we go through in life, our self-esteem changes all the time. Nobody can be 100 per cent strong, 100 per cent of the time. And if they could, we'd certainly think they weren't normal! But if you generally like and accept yourself then you'll be equipped to deal with an awful lot, and to take good opportunity when it comes your way.

It's easy to lose sight of what's going on inside us when we're scurrying about in our hectic lives, worrying about everyday things like paying the rent or what's happening in our social lives, or whether our children are safe and happy. It's all too easy to start to lose touch with who we really are deep down and let all these things in life begin to grind us down, until one day we hardly recognise ourselves.

Before my attack I relied on my good looks to see me through, but as a result I never truly considered who I *was* inside. What was my personality like? Sure, it was bubbly and I liked having a laugh and was determined to try my luck to find fame. But I had no idea what the bigger meaning of my life was. I'd no idea what my boundaries were (I had very few) and I didn't care that much what other people thought of me (which can be both a good and a bad thing). Losing my face prompted me to ask: Who am I really, deep inside? It's a question few of us ask, but when we take the time to know ourselves and our talents and limitations, it can help us focus on the things that make us truly fulfilled.

After I lost my face, I had to find the new Katie. Again, it wasn't something anyone else could do. I had to try to rebuild my self-esteem and re-establish my place in the world, my friendships, the ability to walk out of the front door and be in the world with a very different appearance for people to respond to.

I was initially terrified of what people thought. While I wore my mask in the early days I kept well hidden with a big pair of sunglasses and a big floppy hat. But as I became less fearful, I thought more about what I was saying and how the real me came across. After all, I didn't have my looks to rely on any more. And being a bit older and having gone through a major ordeal, I felt more empathy for other people and what was going on inside them too. Instead of talking so much, I started listening. I started caring more. I wanted to know what made other people tick. I thought about life and the world in a more intelligent and sensitive way, I think. I felt stronger, and more confident in me.

Building or maintaining good self-esteem and learning to check in with ourselves every so often helps keep us connected and in control of our lives, even when everything around us can seem chaotic. It can also give you the confidence to get out there and change your life. It doesn't mean you're going to get too full of yourself, or that your personality will change. In fact, there are a lot of very quiet people I know who rarely call attention to themselves for the very reason that they are at peace with themselves and therefore don't feel a need to fight for attention.

One therapist I worked with said that a simple way of describing self-esteem was that you feel you are 'okay'. She also said that people with good self-esteem have something called 'appropriate regard' for themselves. That is, they do not see themselves as better or worse than other people, and they totally accept that they have as much right to be on this planet as anyone else. Do you feel this way about yourself? I hope so, because you deserve to.

What causes low self-esteem?

Low self-esteem issues all too often come from events or relationships that are rooted in childhood (like a critical parent), or from an abusive relationship of some kind, or from neglect, or just from years of not looking after ourselves very well. The insecurities of our past can become a big part of who we are and how we handle every part of our life. Sometimes, like with me, your self-esteem can be completely knocked by an event that comes from out of the blue. Some people believe that their social status keeps them from feeling confident in all situations; it makes me sad when I hear people say things like, 'I'm only a cleaner, so how can I talk to so and so?' or, 'Nobody in my family went to university, so I guess that's how it'll be for me.' We all have the same human right to happiness, no matter what or where we came from.

My charity received a letter from a girl who wrote that her confidence was knocked after she was bullied in a new job:

'*Dear Katie,*

I started working at a legal firm six months ago and it has been a nightmare in so many ways. At first I was nervous as it was a new position and I struggled with the workload. But then my superior started picking on me and my faults. I literally start to shake before I even get to work and feel sick all day long. I just know whatever I do will always be wrong. I am constantly being criticised and threats have been implied about my 'work behaviour' but no action has been taken.

'It's affected every area of my life. I just feel so useless. Even making a decision like what to have for dinner seems overwhelming now, whereas before I used to be quite an outgoing, confident person. Having watched your documentary, I realise you have had to face some very hard situations and I wanted to get some advice on how to cope with this! Thank you, Lisa.'

What a horrible situation for anyone to be in. To receive constant criticism, whether from a parent, employer or partner, is very demoralising. It takes courage to recognise and accept that someone else's behaviour has affected you like this and then take action to overcome it. But it can be done. Part of that approach involves dealing with your thoughts about the person who hurt you so that you don't slide into victim-thinking.

So, first of all, to help get Lisa out of her crisis we thought about practical steps she could take to protect herself, like investigating legal routes or contacting her HR department to try and stop the bullying and to give her support. After taking these practical steps, Lisa then had to begin to deal with her inner demons.

As I've said, I've tried to challenge my thoughts about people who've not had my best interests at heart. With regards to my attackers, I now just feel sorry for them. And I feel the same way about the people who post negative things about me on Twitter. I think it's very sad that they don't have the strength of mind to think of anything to say but something hurtful. So remember, it's all about how you take control of your feelings – what someone does or how they act towards you may be wrong, but how you deal with it is down to you.

Stop comparing yourself

When we're feeling a blow to our self-esteem, it's very easy to feel envious of other people and all the things they seem to have going for them. As I mentioned earlier, I had to stop comparing myself to all my old modelling friends. Instead of feeling resentment, I'd try to think objectively with things like: 'She looks lovely, and good luck to her with what she's doing.' It wasn't always easy, but it wouldn't do me any good to feel envious of my friends for two reasons – I couldn't change what had happened to me, and what happened to me wasn't their fault.

Avoiding envy can be tricky when we want something good to come into our lives or when we want so much for something to change or go away. I met a woman named Sunita, 31, who felt terrible when all of her friends from university got married within a few years of graduating, something she wanted so much for herself. She said: *'I grew so resentful. It felt so unfair. I'd had boyfriends but my relationships didn't seem to last. And then, one by one, wedding invitations were dropping on my mat and I had to go to each one on my own. I found it torturous. I wanted what they had, but could never seem to find it. I just started hating my life. I knew I was jealous but couldn't seem to stop it.'*

Sunita is proof that if you compare your life to those of other people you will *always* fall short. There is always someone out there with a bigger house, a better job, nicer hair, clearer skin, more money or a lovely boyfriend. But *you are you!* Everyone's life progresses at its own pace. It's important to focus on that and what you do have, otherwise you just waste your energy feeling jealous and give your critical voice too much power. It's a shame that Sunita couldn't go to the weddings with an open mind and simply have fun and enjoy the happiness of her friends. Instead, she tainted her thoughts before she even got there and guaranteed herself a bad time, and then let her jealous feelings continue to eat her up.

I get so many letters from people who suffer from low self-esteem, especially teenage girls, which is made worse by their feelings of insecurity around their peers. I got a letter from a young woman named Nadine, whose concerns about her weight and appearance were causing her extreme anxiety. Sadly, this is such a common concern with young women these days.

> *'Dear Katie,*
>
> *I realise my life could be worse, but actually I can't help but feel I hate myself. Whenever I walk into a room, like at a party or classroom at college, I feel so self-conscious and like every girl in the room is prettier, funnier, or a smaller size than me. It really makes me cringe inside just to walk across a shopping centre sometimes. I feel so shy and alone. I don't know why, but I do. I wish I was two stone lighter, I wish I had more friends, I wish I could afford hair extensions, there is so very much I'd like to change but I can't afford it or can't do it. If I could wake up one day and be someone else I'd jump at the chance. Nadine.'*

Like so many, Nadine is trapped in a mindset where she focuses on things she doesn't have and her inner voice has become deeply critical as a result and constantly comparing herself to others, finding faults. The reality is that Nadine can't see what she *does* have going for her. She has lots of friends, she is very bright and expects to do well in her exams. But by continually comparing herself negatively to her peers she will only notice the things she doesn't have and will never feel content.

> **'The race is long, and in the end, it's only with yourself.'** Baz Luhrmann

Celebrity and the Media: life isn't as perfect as it seems!

It's not just our friends that we compare ourselves to – so many people spend too much time obsessing about celebrities and how they look and live. I get many letters from young people who aspire to fame, asking me how to get there. We're forever bombarded by images in the media of 'perfect' beauty, which makes us feel like our own body and life is imperfect and out of place. But in fact, the opposite is true. Most of the images we see in the media of models and movie stars are completely false!

Most people are aware that photos in magazines, newspapers and online have often been airbrushed, but I think few know to what extent. I've been airbrushed many times, and although I now ask not to be I understand that magazines want everyone to look polished and perfect to sell copies. They also have countless stylists and makeup artists and assistants – and, tell me, what average person has all these things in their life? Even these models and supermodels get spots and have cellulite and relationship problems and rotten days where nothing goes right. No amount of fame can protect them from a surprise illness or a death in the family or a pregnancy that goes wrong or any number of things that we all have to face in life – I promise you. The only difference is that for a few minutes or hours, they make it *look* like it does.

It was quite funny one evening when I took a friend of mine to an awards ceremony. She spotted a reality TV star and nearly choked on her drink with shock. 'She looks about ten years older in real life and so different!'

I couldn't help but laugh. 'That's what airbrushing does for you!' I replied.

I felt pretty sad though, too. We so often get trapped comparing ourselves to a version of reality that is in no way real. Some letters I've received are from girls who are unhappy with their skin. One of them even hated the pores on her skin so much that she felt terrible about leaving the house – it was something that nobody but her would ever notice but she couldn't do anything but compare herself to her idea of perfection.

When images are airbrushed to the extent you cannot see a single blemish or even the pores on the skin, it's inevitable people might get confused about what is normal and what isn't. Having spots and open pores on your skin is *completely normal*.

Too many of us aspire to look like something which just doesn't exist. It's almost like wishing you looked like an animation like Lara Croft or have a waist like Jessica Rabbit! No one in the world can look like that as we are living breathing (sweating!) human beings. If you compare yourself to these images you're setting yourself up for failure. So what can we do? Well, we all love looking at these magazines and awards shows, there's no reason to stop, but instead of thinking, 'Why am I not like that?' try to simply enjoy the entertainment. Have fun looking at their dresses and hair, enjoy looking at the crazy outfits models wear with your girlfriends, but draw the line with yourself when you start to believe the fantasy and want to become anyone other than who you already are.

Beware: social media can make you envious!

Have you ever logged onto Facebook and thought: 'Gosh, everyone is having a more exciting time than me!'? You're certainly not alone in thinking this. When your friends and acquaintances post amazing holiday snaps and share pictures of their gorgeous weddings, or joyfully declare to the world that they are pregnant, it can leave you feeling inadequate or discontent with your own life – but only if you let it!

Remember that people tend to post their best, happiest, most fun-filled pictures, where they like how they look and want to show off what they're doing or where they are. You rarely see status updates like: 'I am having a rubbish time, my life is boring.' Don't assume that people's lives are perfect just because that's what you see online – and don't waste your time trying to measure up – what you see online is a fantasy version of everyone's lives. There is always other life-stuff going on behind the scenes that you just don't know about. Everyone has a house to clean and taxes to file and school runs to do and planes that were late, not to mention the really hard stuff in life like divorce or redundancy or depression.

So if you find that social media is making you feel insecure, simply try to minimise the amount of time you spend on it. It really is as simple as that. If it isn't good for you, just slow down or stop! I know this can be easier said than done, but you have to be disciplined if you want to feel better, and I promise life will not pass you by if you don't look at Facebook for two days. This is especially true if you're prone to low self-esteem. If you simply can't stop looking and checking social media sites even though they're making you feel awful, then you have to work hard to keep everything in perspective and remember: what you see is absolutely not 100 per cent real life.

Know your boundaries – finding the limits of what you will and won't tolerate

Do you find yourself always taking on other people's responsibilities for them, either at home or at work – you know, the stuff they should be doing for themselves? Do you volunteer to take on too much in your life for fear that saying no will make others not like you? Do you see your own life slipping away because you're spending so much time trying to make others happy? Do you feel you pay too many compliments and try too hard to make people like you? Do you just put up with it when people treat you badly because you're afraid you'll upset them?

You may feel this is the way you've been for years and years and have come to see this as how you are, and that you're just being nice. You may feel that being the one everyone comes to for help is your role in life (and you get very little back in return). But part of self-confidence is knowing and recognising your ability to set healthy limits both for yourself and other people.

Boundaries are based on our morals (the things we think are right or wrong) and our standards of how we want to behave and how we want to be perceived by our peers. How others react to us depends on these boundaries. We need to know what our boundaries are, to stay firm about our own basic needs in relationships and friendships, and we need to be confident that 'no' is sometimes the most positive thing we can say!

Our boundaries can sometimes become blurred – that is, we don't know how to stop people crossing the line with us, and we don't speak up about what isn't acceptable to us. We might find ourselves allowing people to disrespect us, or we may notice we constantly seek unhealthy relationships (whether friendships or sexual/romantic relationships), and ultimately end up feeling used. It can make our behaviour quite reckless at times. But the one thing to pay attention to in all these cases is that if these things are happening over and over, if you feel you're constantly being taken advantage of, or that the people in your life simply don't care enough about you, the one common factor in all of that...is *you*. And once you realise that the way you're being treated can so often be down to how you allow yourself to be treated, then you can start to turn it around. This doesn't let others off the hook for not treating you with respect, but it's far easier to respect someone who respects themselves. Saying 'no' can sometimes be the best way of gaining respect.

> **'Nobody can hurt me without my permission.'**
> Mohandas Gandhi

For example, I knew a woman who was so afraid of hurting her friends' feelings that she became everyone's 'yes' person. Whenever anyone wanted her she went running to help. It made her feel good to be needed, but she didn't set appropriate boundaries and she did things like give money to people she didn't know well, took time off work to look after other people's kids, which put her job at risk, let someone live in her house rent-free and never complained when they didn't pull their weight around the house or even thank her. Though she felt taken advantage of, she didn't want to hurt anyone's feelings. She didn't speak up and start to set limits until she had a wake-up call and found she had run out of money. It took a lot of courage, but when she was able to start responding to her friends' requests with polite answers like, 'I can't lend you money but I'm happy to help you find a job online,' or, 'I can babysit your kids if you can look after mine next week,' or simply, 'I would love to help you, but I can't right now,' (and then stick to her decision), she realised that she didn't lose friends. Some were surprised by this change in her, but nobody thought the worse of her, and she discovered that her newfound confidence even attracted people into her life who were less needy.

I've had to be very careful to set boundaries in my own life. Certainly, the men who attacked me went so far over the line as to be violent and criminal in their actions, but that's a very different sort of boundary that they crossed. The boundaries I deal with now on an everyday level have more to do with the fact that it is so important to me to help people, and so many people reach out to me for help. My heart says to go and visit each and every person and hold their hand as they get better. But this is simply a physical impossibility and would keep me from being strong enough to help anyone. I wouldn't have the time or strength to run my charity or do other things to help people, like writing this book. So the boundary I set is not with the people who ask for help (I always want people to know they can write to me at my charity) but with myself – I have to set limits about how much I can do. I try to respond to everyone who contacts me, as it's so important that I do, but instead of trying to do their recovery for them, I aim to help give them the resources to do it themselves, or point them towards professionals who can give them the regular support that they need. That way, I can keep helping more people. This is the thing that means most to me in my personal life.

If someone crosses the line with you, like making you do things you don't want to do (not just irritating things like lending money, but more disruptive things like pressuring you to drink, steal, lie or have sex before you're ready) or makes you feel bad about yourself for any reason, be as confident as you can on *your* side of the boundary and be clear that it is not acceptable to you. Being assertive (not aggressive, just assertive) and knowing what sort of people we do and do not want in our lives becomes easier with practice, and the outcome in the long term is a more peaceful and productive existence, with more time for you to get on with the things that bring you happiness.

In his book *How to Mend Your Broken Heart*, Paul McKenna describes having a 'Me' club, imagining he is the boss of himself and his life and how if someone is very rude or unpleasant towards him he simply 'evicts' them from his club and has little to do with them, rather than starting an argument or getting upset. I quite like this idea!

Of course, as you gain confidence in your ability to say no, be careful not to just cast people out of your life because you experience conflict. Your relationships are important; it's not about simply replacing the people in your life with those who fit in better. Our relationships can change all the time and conflict can be resolved with a little work on both sides. It is possible to be flexible with boundaries and push them in a positive way, but often if something doesn't 'sit right' with us or feel good, it means it isn't, so try to recognise the difference between conflicts you can resolve, and those you can't (like with those people who may be abusive and who won't get help for it).

Just as other people can step over the line with us, we can also cross other people's boundaries in all kinds of ways. Have you ever been at a party and found yourself next to someone who doesn't stop talking about themselves and comes across actually as rather arrogant and awkward? As much as being cripplingly shy can be socially uncomfortable, so can gabbling your life story to anyone who will listen, and it can be a real turnoff. If you tend to do this, try to catch yourself and stop. We don't always do it because we're egotistical (though some certainly do!), we often do it because we just want people to like us. We try too hard to win them over.

As I mentioned earlier, I used to tell my story to anyone who would listen. I'd give far too much of myself and then feel resentful and manipulated when people asked me question after question about the attack, how it felt, what happened, etc. I'd leave a room feeling both exhausted and violated. But I had invited it because I just wanted people to like me, and I didn't know how to stop them from asking so many questions without hurting their feelings. So if people stared at my scars, I'd launch into what happened, whether I actually wanted to or not (or whether they wanted to hear it or not!).

An old colleague of mine named Wendy is someone who understands what I am talking about. She's suffered chronic low self-esteem her whole life because of her mother's harsh criticism and judgement of her when she was a child. As she grew up, she craved other people's approval, and her identity was so wrapped up in her relationships that she would cling on to them tightly and talk about her boyfriend to whoever would listen.

'I found myself dating a singer in a band when I was younger and whenever anyone asked (and often even when they didn't!) I just launched into this whole talk about how amazing he was, and gave all the details of our relationship, even to strangers. I guess I thought it must validate what a good person I must be if someone like him wanted to be with me. But looking back, the reality is that people must have thought I was a bit vulnerable or a show-off!'

Your life, your choices and your experiences are yours. You don't 'owe' anyone any explanations. Trust your instincts. If telling someone about an event in your life doesn't feel good any more, then it probably isn't.

Showing your confidence

Earlier in the book, I mentioned the 'fake it till you make it' approach as a way to drag yourself up from rock bottom and put on a positive face. But it's also really important here – the best advice I have for anyone who wishes they felt more confident in themselves is, again, just to pretend! Seriously. I have followed this advice throughout most of my recovery, and it is something I always come back to when I'm out of my comfort zone. I've been in some hideous situations, like walking into a restaurant while wearing my mask and everyone staring at me, or being stopped in the street by a stranger asking: 'What happened to your face?' And every time, I'd take a deep breath, plaster a smile across my face and hold my head high.

Of course, when I did this the first time in that restaurant, I didn't believe it would actually work. I thought I was just acting, I even pretended that I was. When I was almost having a panic attack, I remembered what it was like to work as a TV extra (I was once in a scene in *EastEnders*!) so I imagined that I was on set. I made myself 'go through the motions', as if I was someone else just pretending to be me, until I could breathe more easily. After a few times of putting on this brave face, it eventually became mine.

I still get stared at in the street and some people even point – and not because they recognise me from television. They just see my scars. I have learned to deal with this by catching their eye and giving them a big, toothy smile! Instead of cowering with embarrassment like I used to, I turn the attention back onto them. Often they will either smile back genuinely and the awkward moment passes, or they will give an 'embarrassed' smile, but either way I've let them know in my own way that I'm okay with myself. So if you want to be a more confident person, try it on for a while by just pretending to be more confident. Wear it around and see how it feels. It just might stick.

You can also show your confidence by choosing to walk away from a situation you're not happy in – for example when your boundaries are being crossed. Whether you are on a date and don't want to kiss the guy at the end (even if he does!) or have a scar you're not happy talking about, then having self-confidence helps avoid uncomfortable situations where you end up feeling powerless and shaky. Confidence is about knowing what you want and don't want and being able to communicate this effectively.

Finally, know that low self-esteem can cause your negative inner voice to start up. We talked about negative noise in Chapter 5, and how it can stand in the way of positivity. Well, it can also sap your confidence, so get into the habit of recognising it and turning it off. For example, on a date with a boyfriend, I found myself consumed with worry about what would happen when I met his friends. 'What if they look at me and wonder why he's going out with someone with burns?' I thought. 'What if they ask him why he couldn't meet someone "normal"?' These days, I am well practised at recognising my negative noise, so in this instance I decided to speak back to myself: 'Your new boyfriend is an adult and can make up his own mind, Katie,' I said. 'His friends are probably very nice so just imagine it going brilliantly and then it's more likely to happen.' I started to feel better and more confident pretty much straight away. Of course, you can't always just snap your fingers and feel immediately confident. You have to work on it. And again, it might feel a bit fake at first, but if you do it often enough, the confidence will soon sink in.

Unhealthy confidence boosters

Sometimes it's tempting to rely on quick fixes to boost your self-confidence – and I am certainly no stranger to this. After two glasses of wine, everyone can feel a bit more relaxed, more sociable, more confident. But you know as well as I do that this is just a transitory feeling. It's not from your heart, so it's not a proper answer to your issues. Other people shop to soothe themselves, some get cosmetic surgery, some crash diet, others seek out social situations to the point of exhaustion for fear of being on their own. Each of these things is no problem in itself (there's nothing wrong with feeling good about socialising, having a drink, losing a few pounds or treating yourself to a new pair of shoes) and you certainly shouldn't beat yourself up if these things make you feel better, but if you find yourself turning to these things too often because you're feeling low, try to challenge your thinking and ask yourself if you're doing it for the right reasons.

Other people have more damaging ways of making themselves feel better or more important, like insulting, criticising or controlling others. Often they don't even realise they're doing this. Nobody wants to be that kind of person, so take care that it's not something you're doing unwittingly. Listen to the things you say or the things that make you react. If you find yourself picking on others when you feel bad about yourself, you'll need to get control of that pretty quickly before it escalates. Once you start to work on the core of what makes you happy (which does take time, and often needs some professional help), then you'll start to gain healthy control of your feelings and behaviour.

Instant confidence boosters

If you need a confidence boost right now, avoid the quick fixes and try these simple tricks! Trust me, they work.

o **Stand tall.** Sounds so simple, right? Confident people don't slouch, and standing straight makes you more alert and aware. Try it.

o **Focus on the positive.** Take time to think of a few things that have gone right for you and allow yourself to enjoy the achievement.

o **Pretend you're on stage.** If you act confident, you're more likely to feel and become confident.

o **Rethink it!** When your confidence is getting beaten, stop and consider how it can be turned on its head. Sometimes, even now, if someone stares at me I say loudly to myself in a funny way: 'It's because they fancy me!' It might sound crazy, but it really works. Your subconscious will listen if you tell it enough times.

o **Get active.** Getting out of breath is scientifically proven to boost your mood. Like it or not, exercise is a much better option than drinking alcohol or taking recreational drugs as it's a 'safe' high, beats depression and will make you feel good for longer. Do you need to be convinced further?

Having self-confidence and a belief in yourself is not about being arrogant or selfish. It is all about being at peace with yourself and having an inner knowledge that you are okay and that you can make good decisions for yourself. It will help guide you on a path in life that is good for you, and will help you to know that whatever happens in your life, you'll have the strength to pull through and thrive.

Points to help you believe in yourself:

o **Good self-esteem is a powerful tool in life** – it will equip you to deal with all sorts of situations and give you the confidence to seize opportunities when they come your way.

o **Low self-esteem often isn't your fault.** It may have been caused by how other people have treated you, or by traumatic or troubling events. While you can't change the past or control other people, you *can* take charge of your feelings and reactions.

o **Know your boundaries.** If you're clear about what you will and won't tolerate in life, other people are more likely to accept that and treat you respectfully.

o **Speak up!** If someone crosses your line, don't be afraid to say no – you don't owe anyone anything. Be ready to tell people what you *do* want. Confidence is about knowing what you want and deserve, and being able to communicate it effectively.

o **Put on a brave face.** Acting confidently can work wonders when you're out of your comfort zone. Even if you're quaking inside, a brave face will trick others – and yourself – into believing your confidence is real.

o **Choose the right confidence boosters.** Stand tall, get active and challenge your thinking. Turn your back on quick-fixes and unhealthy habits – they might make you feel great for five minutes but they won't do you much good in the long run.

CHAPTER 13

Leading a purposeful life: find meaning in all that you do

We have all asked ourselves at some point: 'Why am I here?' Maybe in dark times you've even said, 'What's the point of my life?' Finding what makes you feel needed or important and having a sense that you have a purpose in this world is so important to your happiness and wellbeing. It's what helps get you out of bed in the morning, ready to take on the world and feeling like you have everything to live for. When life throws us a curve ball, this is what gives us a solid foundation to cope with anything.

There are all kinds of things that help give us this feeling. My charity certainly makes me feel I'm leading a meaningful life, as does my close relationship with my family. For you it may be your job, volunteering, being creative, your education, even being a good parent or friend. Here we'll look at the things that help give us this sense of meaning, why it makes us feel so good, and how good role models can help keep us on track.

'Begin each day as if it were on purpose.'
Mary Ann Radmacher, motivational author

A sense of purpose is vital to your happiness– find yours!

When you're facing rock bottom, or just feeling frustrated and hopeless in a particular area of your life, like dating, dieting or job hunting, it's all too easy to focus on your 'flaws' and the things you don't do very well. But these are exactly the times when you need to pay attention to the things that you *do* do well and the things that bring you even a little bit of joy.

You may be stuck in a rut of negative thinking, believing that nothing works and that you've run out of things to try, or that it's all too intimidating, but sometimes you just need to start small. Like when you count your blessings when things go wrong in life, you end up counting the things you took for granted. It's the same with finding your sense of purpose, you may simply not be paying attention to the things you succeed at because you're too caught up in the things that aren't going so well. Once you start to focus on those positives, you'll find that one thing leads to another, that your strength builds and you feel more confident to go out and tackle bigger goals, little by little, and you will feel more and more connected to the world in a really healthy way.

Every single one of us is good at *something;* something you can use to carve a path for yourself into the future. You may simply be putting too much pressure on yourself about what you *should* be doing or *could* be doing instead of looking a little closer at what you *are* doing. Look hard, you may find things that aren't obvious at first glance. You might be terrible academically but have an amazing ability to listen to your friends and give them comfort.

You might be a terrible cook and awful at keeping the house clean, but brilliant at entertaining kids, or you're great with animals. And to be honest, these are the things that really matter in life, not whether you're perfect or beautiful or rich or famous or have the best job. Remember, you don't have to be a superhero, so give yourself a break. Focus on asking yourself, 'What am I good at? What can I offer?' And the answer is: lots and lots, so don't stop looking until you have the answer.

When I was in recovery I could have applied for long-term disability benefit. It would have covered the cost of me having my own house and I could have lived the rest of my life being financially supported. But I was told that if I claimed it I'd not be allowed to do any work at all, not even volunteering, and for me this wasn't an option. I couldn't sit at home not letting my life happen when I felt so strongly that I wanted to make a contribution to the world. I was incredibly grateful that financial help was available, and so many people really do critically need it, but it just didn't feel right for me. Plus, I could hardly wait to get out there and make up for lost time. I didn't know how, but I had to have the option to do *something*. So I chose not to claim the benefit – and I guess I might have ended up a very different person if I'd opted for that route in life, as I would never have had the opportunity to set up my charity.

So, I began to think about what I had to offer, what skills or interests and abilities. I saw it as an opportunity to find what I *wanted* to do and where I would be most useful. When we feel needed and useful, it gives so much meaning and contentment. As I've said, we *all* have something to offer. Even if you don't feel you have a particular talent, your time and energy is something so precious and from there, you may find whole new worlds open up for you.

Whatever it is you're doing, whether you're at home cleaning all day, looking after a baby, sweeping the streets or studying for a PhD, if you take pride in what you're doing (even if it seems really hard to) then you'll actually start to enjoy it more. Being able to say: 'I did that well' gives a sense of satisfaction, which you can then build on.

I knew a girl, Tracy, who was convinced she wasn't good at anything. 'Nothing at all?' I pressed. 'No!' Tracy cried. 'I flunked all my exams, I don't like reading books and I am no good at sport. There is nothing for me. I've tried loads of things but I'm rubbish at them all.'

'But what do you *like* doing?' I asked. 'There must be at least one little thing!'

Eventually Tracy admitted she loved baking. Even though she didn't do it very often it was something she enjoyed. A month later, one of our fundraisers persuaded her to join a cake stall to raise money for the Foundation. Tracy made boxes of the most delicious cakes and single-handedly raised £100, which was brilliant, and the pride she took in it made her feel and act like a different person! Not only did this success make her smile, but it also helped her to see what *was* actually possible and helped her to break out of her self-defeating mindset.

Having a sense of purpose can mean almost anything you wish it to. When I had to testify against my attackers in court I was terrified and didn't want to do it, but I thought to myself: 'It is my *purpose* to do this.' I didn't want anyone else to suffer a similar attack. I didn't want these guys to take things even further and kill some poor girl. For a time, my 'purpose' in life became to make sure they were put behind bars. That may be an extreme example, but it was one way to look at my immediate life to make sense of what was happening to me, and to help give a reason to fight for my new self.

You can make a difference! Helping others will help you find a sense of purpose

When life is busy – with work or college, social life, family, and all our day-to-day trials and tribulations – it's easy to lose sight of the fact that we're part of a much bigger picture. We might think: 'No one will notice if I don't do this, or don't bother with that.' But that's not always true. In fact, you can make a huge difference, either all on your own or as part of a group. I think the cleanup operation after the London riots was a fantastic example of this. A man whose street was vandalised during the rioting posted on Twitter urging people to get together the next morning to help put their neighbourhood back together. Hundreds of people arrived for the mass clear up – all because of this one man! He had seen a big problem and decided to find a solution, and everyone who turned up felt a sense of goodwill and accomplishment for helping their neighbours. They could easily have done nothing, either because they didn't believe they could make a difference or because they felt it wasn't their responsibility, but instead something brilliant happened.

When I found that there were few resources to give support to or help burns victims make a positive recovery, I could easily have done nothing about it. I could have thought 'If only someone would start a burns charity,' and assumed that someone *else* would do it. But I was determined that things should change and that society would be more understanding about the way I looked – and others like me. I was also determined to help people, so I started the charity myself. We can all make a difference! Of course I don't mean that you have to go as far as starting your own organisation, I just want to remind you that the little things *do* count.

I had a letter from a woman called Lucy, 24, who had just finished university and couldn't find a job she wanted. So instead of simply sitting around waiting for things to happen, she signed up to volunteer in her local area through a website.

'At first I just felt really nervous. I'd never volunteered for anything in my life! But then I started to get unpaid work on an allotment helping local school kids plant a vegetable patch. It was so much fun! I knew almost nothing about gardening before but I learned how to plant all kinds of seeds. It was so rewarding but also made me feel great that I was helping out the school. After being stuck at home unemployed, it gave me some structure and something to get up for in the morning. The bonus was that I loved it too. After six weeks, I decided that actually, I'd love to become a teacher. Something I'd never ever considered before.'

Lucy is positive proof that just by taking a simple action, she not only felt fulfilled and worthwhile but she also found a purpose in life where she least expected it. So if you are struggling to find a single purpose for your life, don't let it worry you, just try something that you like the sound of – even if you're not sure *how* it's 'purposeful'- and see where it leads you. By doing something, anything, you can often find the inspiration to do the thing that perhaps you were meant to do. You may not find your purpose until you get out there and explore a few different avenues.

I constantly find new inspiration from the people I meet through my charity, and one in particular was a lady in her 50s who told me that for 20 years she had suffered domestic violence at the hands of her husband. She was beaten or hit almost daily and feared for her life if she left him. Then finally, one day she confided in a friend, who helped her find the strength to leave and took her to a safe house. She then moved to a refuge for people who had suffered domestic abuse. When she finally came out the other side of her horrific ordeal, she decided that her new purpose in life would be to help anyone else who was suffering in the way that she had. She set up her own refuge for victims of domestic violence with the aim of helping people leave their dangerous partners much earlier than she did. I found her story so amazing - she'd gone from victim, to survivor, to rescuer. How inspiring!

One little thing I did in the French rehab centre not only made me feel wonderful and needed, but also led to bigger things. When I first started trying new camouflage makeup to cover my scars, I hated having to use it. But then I grew in confidence and of course the beautician in me started to enjoy it, and then other female burns survivors at the centre asked me what prescription makeup I was using. After a few months I found myself inviting some of them to my room and giving an impromptu makeup class! Soon I had loads of girls who had burns and scars coming to my classes. It was not only helping people, but it was a lot of fun too! Now my charity runs a workshop teaching people with scars how to apply makeup and survivors travel from across the country to attend. And it all started from my little room in France!

> **'Not all of us can do great things. But we can do small things with great love.'** Mother Teresa

Think about what your purpose is today. Are you passionate about your job? Are you a parent? Are you someone's sister? Friend? Colleague? What can you do for them today? As grateful as I was for all the support my family gave me, little did I know I was in turn also supporting them by trying to remain positive and cheerful. Sometimes the fastest way towards finding a sense of purpose (and getting out of rock bottom) is to look outside yourself and towards others that you can help, even when you feel like you're the one who needs all the support. You can make people feel good about themselves or provide support when times are tough, or simply be the one to make them smile. Believe me, one sure-fire way of feeling happier is to bring happiness to other people! It's something we can forget all too easily in our hectic modern world where there is so much emphasis on what job you do, how much money you earn, your material possessions and of course your *own* happiness.

Many studies have revealed that the happiest people are the ones who volunteer. My mum is a great example of this. When I was a kid, she was always helping elderly neighbours with their shopping, taking ill friends to hospital or babysitting for someone.

Almost every single day she was busy doing something, and I just assumed that's what all mums did. My mum is pretty special that way, she is such a giving, caring person, and what she does for others makes her feel useful, needed and valued.

Of course, nowadays so many of us have very busy lives, working and looking after our own families, so it may be that you only have a few hours a week or possibly per month that you can spare to help others. It doesn't matter how much or how little time you give to your community or charities, every little bit makes a big difference to the people who run them and the people who receive help from them. So think about what you can do to help others, whether lending a hand at the school fete, spending time at a drop-in centre or charity, or just offering to walk your neighbour's dog. Doing something for someone else can help in two ways:

○ It makes us feel grateful for what we do have in our lives
○ It makes us feel valuable for making someone else's life a little brighter.

Sometimes you can use your own experience to help others, like Pam Warren did for me. Maybe you have suffered some abuse (like physical or sexual), or have an addiction or eating disorder, or perhaps your childhood wasn't as happy as you'd have liked it to be, or you were dumped out of the blue by your long-term partner. Or maybe you just know someone in one of these situations and it's taught you a lot. If you or someone close to you has benefited from the help of others, perhaps you'd like to give back and help make a real difference to someone else, particularly if you have an understanding of what they are going through.

Volunteering with specific organisations can be cathartic and really help you to move on from your own situation, too, as well as giving you a sense of self-worth and purpose in your life. If the idea of helping others who have suffered the same experiences as you seems daunting – perhaps because you feel that your experiences have left you too raw and exposed to help people on a face-to-face level at first – perhaps see if you can help behind the scenes until you feel confident enough to face your demons. Remember, finding a purpose in your life is a part of your recovery and it too is all about taking little steps to reach the end goal.

When you're feeling fragile about your experiences and situation you should beware of the difference between helping other people because it makes you feel genuinely happy and gives you a sense of purpose, and trying too hard to make other people like you by doing things for them. Also be careful if you're the kind of person who already takes on too much because you're always the person who says, 'yes, I'll do that for you', like the woman I mentioned in Chapter 12, who ended up having given too much of her time and money away to others and had to radically change her attitude towards helping. If we identify ourselves too much by what other people think of us, then it's all too easy to lose ourselves. People won't think badly of you if you establish boundaries about how far you will go to give or help – being willing to help at all makes you a special person to them. It's a fine balance to keep, but one that is essential and people will respect you for.

Role models can help you discover your sense of purpose

We all need role models in our lives, those people who we look up to and who inspire us to be the best we can be. From thinking about our role models and the positive things they do, we can start to find inspiration for the things we want in our own lives.

Earlier I mentioned not comparing ourselves negatively to celebrities and famous people, but following the lives of people in the public eye doesn't have to be a negative thing. Some people are famous for the incredible things they have achieved, and some people use their fame to do good in the world and raise awareness for issues that otherwise would not be highlighted without the media attention on those 'stars'.

We can learn from those people who have achieved amazing things and try to apply the positive things they teach us to our own lives, such as the deaf and blind Helen Keller, who went on to be an important political campaigner and author, but we can also be inspired by people who demonstrate their strong characters to the world, and their confidence to be the people they want to be, and who stand by their own beliefs. Some of my favourite modern role models are girls with attitude! I love Fearne Cotton and Holly Willoughby, who don't conform quite so much to a 'type' and have their own strong sense of humour and style. Having my own style is important to me too. I feel I can still look good, even with my scars, by focusing on my smile, on my clothes, and by carrying myself in a way that shows people I'm proud of myself. My own 'attitude' means my scars don't matter so much to me, and in turn, they won't matter so much to other people.

Lorraine Kelly is also an inspiration to me. Her MBE is well deserved in my opinion. She's had a long and successful career, is very down to earth and hasn't needed to resort to being rude or bitchy or grabbing headlines to achieve it. I love that! Deborah Meaden from *Dragon's Den* is also inspirational. She's a big hitter in the business world and has earned the respect of so many others, and has never been afraid to be a strong woman. I think Sarah Brown is another great role model, too, having managed to achieve a successful career in her own right despite being married to a very powerful man. She isn't just seen as 'the woman behind the man', and she does important charity work. She often gets overlooked, I think, and undeservedly so, but watching her be independent and charity-minded has meant a lot to me.

People who devote their lives to helping others are some of my biggest heroes. Nawal El Saadawi is an Egyptian feminist and writer who at 80 years old is still working as a peace activist. She recently returned from campaigning for the rights of Muslim women in Cairo. Even at this age she displays such courage and passion for what she believes in. What an inspiration! I've also heard stories about amazing female paramedics who have helped badly injured soliders in Afghanistan. We rarely hear about the doctors (and even more rarely the nurses) who work tirelessly to save our soldiers' limbs and lives.

But the very best role models in my life have been the people close to me who have taught me so much about how to live my own life just by letting me watch how they live theirs. My top roles models are: my mum (for her kindness, and ability to be there for me), my doctor (for his incredible positive thinking), my ambassadors at my charity (for overcoming their own battles and scars) and lots of other people I come into contact with via charity events – strong survivors who have beaten the odds. Your role models could be your parents, your pastor, your work colleague, your best friend, even people you've never spoken to like the lady down the road who you see helping older people.

Whoever you choose to be your inspiration, they don't have to be glamorous, wealthy or famous, the best role models will just make you take a step back from your own life and make you think, 'What can I do that will give me a sense of purpose'? It doesn't have to be just one person, perhaps there are elements from many people around you that you find inspiring and want to emulate? You can create the person you want to be by piecing together all these qualities.

Whatever stage you are at in your recovery, finding a sense of purpose will guide you through to a whole new life and perhaps a whole new you. Don't put pressure on yourself and feel that your purpose has to be something amazing and inspirational, just start by choosing to do something that matters to you, and you will soon find that it matters to someone else too.

To have come through your experience proves that you have strength and the will to survive; these are amazing qualities that show that you are an important person in the world, with so much to give to all those around you. Find that purpose and you will find happiness and confidence to be the new you.

Points to help you find meaning and purpose in your life:

o **You can build a happier new you.** Having a sense of purpose in the world and feeling valued in life are the cornerstones of a happy life.

o **You matter in this world.** If you think what you do or don't do doesn't count then think again! Everyone has something to offer. Sometimes it just takes a while to discover what that thing is.

o **Draw on your experiences.** Give support to those who have supported you and use your knowledge and experiences to help others in similar situations. You will feel immense pride and self-worth at being able to make a difference in someone else's life.

o **Be inspired by the people around you.** Find the role models in your life who will help give you the courage to find your own path in life. They don't have to be rich or famous (though they may be), they can often come from unexpected places, or be right under your nose!

CHAPTER 14

Getting help

Being able to ask for and find help – whether from books, from those around us or from professionals – is a sign of strength. There is no way I could have got through my worst times had I not accepted and trusted the experts around me, both the doctors and mental health professionals. There is no shame whatsoever in needing and asking for help, and if there is one thing I could do for the world it would be to remove any stigma about something so vital to people's wellbeing. Here we look at how important it is to allow yourself to be helped, what the best help may be for you and how to go about asking for it. You are not alone in needing help and support.

There is always help somewhere: don't be afraid to ask

When a problem has arisen or your emotions have erupted, it can feel like you're wading through treacle: uphill, backwards and even blindfolded sometimes! It can be so overwhelming when you don't know which way to turn, and at times even supposedly 'small' problems can snowball into bigger, unmanageable ones that consume us with stress or fear, or that keep us from functioning properly in our daily lives. The support and sympathy of our loved ones can go a very long way, but if things have got out of control, or if the weight of your feelings has made it too hard to cope, or if you've been stuck in self-defeating patterns, then it's probably time to take a deep breath and look to experts who really do know how to support you and teach you the skills to pull through.

Asking for help is an absolute sign of strength. It takes real guts to say: 'I recognise I have a problem – I need help!' So if you reach this point, congratulations! Your emotional health is as important as your physical health, but in today's modern world we sadly don't think of it like that. In fact, there's a very good argument that your mind is even more important than your body!

There are so many examples of people who have weak bodies but have overcome them with strong minds, intellect or just a stubborn refusal to give up on life. Helen Keller is one of my favourite role models, as I have mentioned. Helen was born in 1880 and became deaf and blind as a very small child. Due to people's misunderstanding of her disability at that time, she was given no chance of a future and was considered unteachable. Her mother was determined not to give up on her and searched until she found a brilliant teacher for Helen named Anne Sullivan, and incredibly Helen learned to talk by touching people's lips and copying their words. She also learned to read using Braille and ultimately she went on to become the first deaf and blind person to get a university degree in America. She became a rights campaigner, and was an author of many books. How incredible is that?

I also think Professor Stephen Hawking is amazing. He was given just two years to live after being diagnosed in the 1960s with a horrific condition called motor neurone disease. He carried on working as a scientist and professor despite the fact that his body was falling apart. Even though he is confined to a wheelchair and he cannot speak without computer aid, he has achieved worldwide recognition for his amazing theories on the universe and his books are among the biggest ever bestsellers! His strong mind and determination made this possible despite being unable to get out of bed or feed himself since 1974.

Of course, these examples are extraordinary, but they do go to prove that even with failing bodies our minds can overcome even the biggest challenges. For the rest of us, it's a lesson that it's so important for us to protect our minds as much as we can so that we can handle just about anything. It's the way you think that can control how you feel and what you get out of life. You may not realise it, but around one in four people in this country will be affected by mental health issues at some point in their lives. Whether it's a feeling of hopelessness, grief, an eating disorder or body image problem, anxiety or unhealthy fears, these hard feelings are a common part of the human condition and we really are all in this together. If you feel ashamed of your problem please know with absolute certainty that you won't be alone. There will *definitely* be other people suffering from the same thing.

When things are this bad, we really can't go it alone – we have to seek outside help, and it cannot be found in a vacuum away from the world.

How do I know if I need help?

We sometimes find it hard to know when to find help because all too often we think we should be able to handle things on our own, even when we're not handling them so well. Sadly, in our society we're made to feel weak if we seek help. We often think asking for it looks to others like we're being needy or attention-seeking. Whatever it is you are going though, if you think you need help, *you do*. No problem is too big or too small.

Aside from a major crisis, here are some common reasons why people seek help:

o **Unhappiness.** It needn't be full-blown depression you're suffering. You may just not be getting the most out of life and you don't know why.

o **Stress, anxiety and panic.** When we worry excessively, our bodies can go into overdrive, producing adrenaline (that butterfly-in-the-stomach feeling that gets us wound up) when it's not needed. This can cause palpitations, excessive sweating, a feeling of dread in the pit of your stomach or full-blown panic attacks where you might even feel like something terrible is happening to you physically. These symptoms are hard to live with every day but they are completely treatable and manageable with the right mental tools.

o **Phobias.** These are extreme fears that don't always seem to make sense. They can have a profound effect on your life, such as fear of leaving home, fear of dogs, fear of flying, fear of others touching us, even fear of particular objects.

o **Relationship problems.** This is one of the main reasons people seek help. Our relationships are a central part of our lives and when they go wrong it can be hard to focus on everything else we need to do.

o **Feeling life is chaotic or out of control.** A series of events can trigger this feeling, and it can be hard to sort out where to start dealing with this by yourself because everything seems equally frantic.

o **Self-harming behaviour**, such as drinking, overeating, drug abuse, cutting yourself, suicidal thoughts, shouting or losing your temper. It is vital that you get treated. I really urge you to be serious about getting help for these – don't wait. All these behaviours tend to spiral out of control without guidance, but specialised help is there if you look for it. (Please see details on the Samaritans on page 26 and other resources on pages 286–96.)

But whatever your issue is, you are *entitled* to stop suffering in silence and find some peace and contentment. Suffering in silence usually leads to even more problems or a deep-rooted unhappiness that becomes harder and harder to shift. If there's one thing I'd love you to take away from this book it is that there's a way out of whatever you're facing and you are allowed to ask for help.

There's no shame in seeking help

If you're reading this and thinking: 'I need help but don't know how...' or, 'My problem isn't big enough,' please, please read on.

Okay, this is the bit where I can hold your hand. I can tell you: whatever it is you're upset about, whatever you need to do to be happier in life, it *is* possible to find that contentment, because I know that to be true.

When you're in that deep dark place, it's harder than ever to reach out and look for a solution. But just taking a few steps in the right direction can bring so much peace to your life and then you can decide how you can take a more positive path. We can only deal with our problems when we start to root out the cause. If you find you're always getting dumped, or feel haunted by old habits or traumas, or suffer from eating disorders, or are struggling to cope after an accident or illness – whatever it is, you likely need to get to the bottom of it in order to get out of it and change your behaviour.

I was ashamed of asking for help, but I am so glad I did!

The first time it was suggested to me that I talk about what I was going through to anyone outside my family, it just felt totally alien. Soon after my attack I was advised to see a burns psychologist because I was told I had something called post-traumatic stress disorder. Basically, it means experiencing horrible terror and out-of-control feelings after you've either suffered or witnessed an awful event. (My symptoms included jumping at just about anything, having nightmares and flashbacks to the attack, and living in fear that bad things would happen to my loved ones.)

I'd never felt the need to get help before the attack, as I'd always handled things on my own, so I couldn't understand why I needed help now. I was embarrassed and ashamed. Previously I had

So many people are afraid to get help at first. I know a girl, Emma, who suffered from bulimia for five years before she sought proper help.

'I just didn't think it was a big enough problem,' she admits. *'After all, I went to college, took my exams, had a part-time job and looked fairly normal from the outside. I felt terrible inside, but in a way I thought I could pretend it wasn't happening if I didn't talk about it. I felt like I was in control of my obsessive thinking but really it was controlling me. The real wake-up call that made me realise I needed help was when I started to get problems with my teeth. They were rotting from being sick and my dentist noticed, which was shocking – I thought I had been hiding everything so well and I felt "found out". When I broke down in the dentist's*

viewed people who spoke to counsellors as 'weak' or 'unstable'; well, that was my old, immature way of looking at things!

'Why should I talk to a psychologist?' I said. 'It's my face that needs more help!'

I was gutted to think I needed this 'special treatment' from a shrink. 'That's it,' I thought. 'People will think I am officially mental now.'

During my therapy sessions, I had to talk about the rape and the attack, but at first I didn't feel comfortable at all. 'I just want to forget about it now,' I thought. But I had to face it. If I had turned my back, I'd have remained stuck where I was, afraid of the world. Eventually I got used to speaking with my psychologist, and little by little we started to unravel my feelings, and now having come through the other side I have no idea how I would have managed without it. I really mean this.

chair, she was so compassionate and suggested I speak to a professional. Even then I was reluctant. I didn't want to be the girl who couldn't cope. My illness was secret as far as I was concerned. It was embarrassing, but clearly I couldn't hide it any more.'

Thankfully Emma did seek help. She started by finding a reputable charity online called B-eat (www.b-eat.co.uk), a national UK support organisation, which has been around for 20 years, who helped her to deal with her eating disorder and bring her life back under control. It took a while, but it had to start somewhere, and it really helped her.

But before you even get this far, first of all many people often think: 'Do I even need therapy?' As I've mentioned, even I didn't think I did – despite what had happened to me! But I think a pretty good rule of thumb is to ask yourself the following questions, which relate to the thoughts already listed about the reasons people get help:

- Has something very serious happened to me, or am I hurting myself?
- Is my problem interfering with my daily life? Can I not stop thinking about it? Does it prevent me from sleeping or functioning normally?
- Have I gone past the stage where my friends or family are able to help me get sorted? Do I keep having the same conversation with them but we never seem to come up with a solution?
- Are others urging me to seek help?

If the answer to any of these is yes, then it's probably time to seek out the experts, even if you just start with self-help books. But please start somewhere.

What help is out there?

There is so much help available, and much of it is specifically offered for all our different issues and difficulties. When you are considering getting counselling, it can sometimes be very confusing to know which type of therapy you need and what you can expect. I'll try to clear up some of these questions in a bit, but first, let's look at where you can start in your search for help.

Of course, the first port of call can be your trusted friends and close family, who will help you to open up about your problem and see that you have one. Someone close to you might have suffered something similar or might know someone else who has been through the same thing and so can be the voice of experience, or perhaps they can just lend a sympathetic ear. But often your problem may be too hard for them to solve, or too painful for them to help you with, and this is when you need to get some professional help.

As I just said, there are many books out there (and hopefully this one!) that can help, written by professionals, experts or just people who have had the same experiences. You can look online from the privacy of your own home to find one that you think is right for you. Millions of books on various subjects are sold every year offering practical advice, and they can offer reassurance that you are not the first to feel this way.

As well as these sources of information and help there are also many wonderful local, national and international support groups on offer, like AA (Alcoholics Anonymous) who provide regular supportive meetings with other people at various stages in their own recovery – some of who may be battling the worst of their drinking, others may have been sober for years but want to stay on track. Sometimes sharing your problems with strangers might be the last thing you'd like to do, but it can also be very healing and powerful when you are with others who are welcoming and who know how you feel. A problem shared can be halved, and not only can you get great advice from someone with exactly the same issue, but you can also get motivated by seeing how their own lives have improved because of the help they have received. It only takes a quick search on Google to find different charities online who can help you cope. Many have helplines and advice lines that you can ring straight away. I've listed some in the back of this book.

The next stop could be asking for help through your GP, school, college or work place. Do you have a doctor or nurse on site or a sympathetic teacher or tutor you look up to?

So what happens next, when it's time to speak to a counsellor or other professional?

Finding a good therapist and getting started

So you've made the decision that you are ready to speak to a therapist (or you at least want to give it a go). Now, how you do find one?

Before you look, ask yourself, 'What am I hoping to get out of this?' Do you want a better love life, are you having trouble coping, or are you battling addictions or the ghosts of past experiences? Did something terrible happen to you as a child? Are you feeling out of control for no reason? Ultimately, you want to get to the root of your problem, as therapists will have varying specialities.

First off, it is possible to get therapy for free on the NHS, though it can be limited. It can still be a good place to start, but if your GP hesitates, do keep pressing to make it happen. Be strong and keep asking, and be very clear about what it is that's troubling you and don't pretend it's not that big a deal. You've worked up the nerve to get this far, so don't leave it to your doctor to guess what's eating you. Though most GPs are caring and sympathetic, if you have one who isn't as sympathetic as you'd like, don't let that intimidate you. Be persistent, or ask your surgery if you can see a different doctor. This is your mind, your health, so feel brave about asking for help until you get it.

You can also get therapy privately, and do not need to get a referral from your GP (though some insurance companies may ask you to if you have a policy that covers mental health care). Private therapy can be expensive, sometimes very expensive, but don't be afraid to ask if they will take your income into account in their pricing, because a great many do. Some charities also offer therapy at greatly reduced rates, so do investigate and do ask around – sometimes someone you know may be able to make a recommendation. If you do have to pay, though, keep remembering that your sound mind is the best possible investment. You willingly pay for other things that are good for you or that feel good, right? So many girls I see spend a fortune on clothes or hair and makeup, or new phones and handbags, while their insides are churned up and their relationships are falling apart. I believe we should give our minds as much TLC as our bodies. So if you do have the means, even a little, don't rule out paying for help.

When you're first seeking help or are offered an initial appointment, you may find yourself confused by the terminology and what different therapists call themselves. A counsellor and a psychotherapist are pretty much the same thing, as both should be trained in counselling and psychotherapy. It used to be that people calling themselves psychotherapists had had more training than people called counsellors, but now this isn't always the case. A psychiatrist is someone who has qualified as a medical doctor before doing further training in problems of the mind. Psychiatrists are the only therapists who can themselves prescribe medication. Finally, there are psychologists (I saw one of these). These are not medical doctors – instead they have a degree in psychology. Many are academics who don't actually come into contact with patients – those who do treat patients tend to call themselves clinical psychologists or chartered psychologists. Any of these terms should give you confidence that the practitioner is fully qualified and competent. But whoever you're referred to, you can ask them to tell you their professional background and experience. You'd certainly want to make sure a surgeon was qualified before he operated on you, so don't feel awkward asking this. They will have been asked many times before and will respect you for taking it seriously enough to want to know that you're in good hands with them. (In the unlikely event that they respond negatively to the question, that in itself will tell you a lot about them!)

Once you've found some options, ring them to find out when they are available and how much they cost (don't be afraid to negotiate this or tell them what you feel you can afford), and then you can also ask them a few questions and talk to them for a bit to get a sense of how they like to work with their clients. I don't think you necessarily have to like your therapist as a person (this is not about creating a friendship) but you should be able to respect them as a professional and trust they are going to respect and help you.

If you have never talked to a therapist before, you may be worried they will think you are silly, judge what you're saying or not understand. But try to remember that this is their job and they are used to hearing all kinds of stories, and *no matter what you say or reveal,* they will not judge you. In fact, this is one of the most helpful things about therapy: you can say the darkest or most unreasonable things and this person will never think badly of you or get embarrassed or upset. That's quite a bonus! It's just like how a medical doctor is used to seeing naked bodies, so there is nothing to be ashamed of. The chances are your thoughts won't be surprising to them either! It's best to go along with an open mind and don't try and diagnose yourself.

When I began therapy, I started to think of the sessions as time for myself, a time just to focus on my thoughts, feelings, reflections on my day, things I wanted to do, anything. It was an amazing chance to share my deepest innermost thoughts that maybe I couldn't even tell my mum or sister! In fact, I talked about things I wouldn't have been able to talk to my family about – like how worried I was for them and what they were going through – but, in therapy, I could get these things off my chest, which otherwise would have just been bottled up. But therapy was also time to simply get a sense of myself in my new life. It was about all kinds of things, but it was all mine. Amazing.

In fact, you will likely get to the point where you feel that your therapist's four walls are a haven of safety for you, just like I did.

But you will need to be prepared to push yourself beyond your comfort zone, and at a pace that feels right for you. You wouldn't expect a personal trainer at the gym to help you get fit by letting you have a nap, and therapy is exactly the same.

What to do if you can't connect to your therapist

If for some reason after a few sessions you find you haven't clicked with your therapist or the therapy itself, first challenge yourself and ask, 'Am I bailing out just because this is painful?' If you really do feel it's the therapist and not the process, then talk to them about it. Really. Don't just run away or feel obliged to keep going because you're afraid you might hurt their feelings. Therapy is all about you and they want what's best for you. Be brave and tell them why you feel it isn't working. They will help you with this part too. This is hugely empowering in itself because you've looked after yourself in a healthy way by speaking up about something that doesn't feel right, and sometimes talking about it allows you to improve the relationship so you don't have to leave or find a replacement. (That in turn will teach you about speaking up for yourself in all kinds of relationships.) But therapy is your time and possibly your money, so you don't have to spend it on someone you are not comfortable with.

If you do want to continue but want to try another therapist, that's great! Don't be afraid to ask for another one. Believe it or not, your current therapist may even be able to recommend someone else they feel you can work with. Again, do not worry about hurting their feelings, this happens all the time and no good therapist will expect things to work for every single patient. It's a working relationship and they know this. Keep at it until you find the right one!

Remember, if it doesn't work with a therapist, try hard not to be discouraged or feel it was a waste of time and money, as you will have learned a lot just from making the decision that this person wasn't right for you. Please don't let it defeat you. Keep at it!

At the back of this book you'll find a list of organisations and other resources that can guide you towards the help you need. Just have a look. You can take it from there.

Types of therapy

If you start to Google 'therapy', you may find the mind boggling at all the choices, and the odd terminology may seem a little intimidating, but below I've listed some of the most common types of therapies, and how to find the right therapist to help you. Whatever type of therapy you end up using, try and go with an open heart and mind and a belief that things get better, because they can!

CBT (Cognitive Behavioural Therapy)

Wow, that's a mouthful! You may have seen this term and wondered what it means, because it's a very common and incredibly useful therapy. Basically, CBT is about how to be super-aware of your thoughts and feelings the minute they are happening and then it gives you really practical ways to change the way you act, like an emotional toolbox. So, it makes you aware of things like, 'I always get nervous when I speak in public, I'm nervous RIGHT NOW,' or, 'I always eat too much when something upsets me, I am upset and feel like having something to eat RIGHT NOW,' and then when you learn to pay attention to that RIGHT NOW feeling, you can get your toolbox out to deal with keeping you from getting too nervous or eating too much, or whatever it is you're trying not to do. CBT is not about spilling your guts to find out *why* you think and act the way you do (though you may still need to do this too), it's just about *how* you change the way you think and act. So it can really provide some instant relief – phew!

CBT is so common and effective for things like bulimia, depression and anger that nowadays if your GP refers you for NHS counselling, the chances are you will be offered CBT. This type of therapy is often quite brief – you may have just six to twelve sessions to get you on track. There are also computer programmes designed around CBT to help people do things like tackle fears.

I had hypnotherapy that focused on CBT. It was a way of dealing with my past and was very powerful. I was asked to visualise what I was scared of in my head, as if I was watching it in the cinema. Then I put it in a box, locked it, threw it off a cliff and walked away without turning around. Next I imagined a cartoon where door after door banged shut! I threw the key in the sea and walked away. Just visualising this over and over helped me to really walk away from it all and put it behind me.

CBT also helped me understand that I was constantly reacting to situations using the emotional side of my brain, not the logical side. Like when I thought that even though my attackers were jailed they'd somehow hurt my family. This kind of thinking is really common and sometimes it's so hard to distinguish what's logical from what's not when our emotions take over! What I learned in CBT I turned into a life skill that I try and think of every day now. I stop, ask myself, 'Is this right, is this happening, is there evidence for my thoughts and feelings or am I just being emotional?'

By reacting to things less emotionally it means you can learn to stop, count to twenty and take a step back – then react more calmly. Now I never fire off texts to people if I am annoyed, or burst into tears if someone writes something horrible about me on Twitter. It doesn't keep me from being annoyed, it just keeps me from doing something I'll regret because I'm annoyed.

Mindfulness as a part of CBT

I've talked about this technique before. Many CBT therapists help their patients focus on 'mindfulness' as well as offering more conventional therapy. It is also commonly used in pain relief and with various other physical problems, as well as in the treatment of eating disorders.

Mindfulness is a technique that really worked for me. It is a lot like Eastern meditation, and lets you give your entire attention to what's happening right now. It's a mixture of meditation, and breathing, and being aware of things as they really are, as opposed to how we'd like them to be.

Many of us make any mental distress – or indeed pain or other trauma – worse by trying to escape from it. But this just adds to our tension and can actually increase the bad feelings we are trying to avoid. Mindfulness is a way of 'being' with the problem. And of being 'curious' about it. And this puts us in a much better position to start looking at how to fix it.

Psychodynamic therapy (also called 'talking therapy')

No, this doesn't mean it's for psychos! This is therapy where the therapist listens to you more than they talk, and it helps by letting you see where your thoughts take you. The therapist will occasionally shed light on what you are saying and what this might mean to you emotionally, or gently guide you to pay attention to your negative thinking, or help to put the pieces of your life together. You will probably talk a lot about your past, and how that may be colouring how you are dealing with life in the present.

Don't worry, this sort of therapy doesn't mean you have to lie on a couch! Well, unless you want to... This kind of therapy will more often than not take place in a comfortable space where you can feel safe, face to face with your therapist. It is a longer-term process, and you and your therapist will decide together what your goals are and how long you need. You don't have to have an end goal (such as deciding that you'll only do it for three months); with talking therapy you go until you feel you're ready not to, though your therapist will help you figure out when that is. This could be months, or years, depending on how deep your issues lie or how tricky your behaviours are to resolve. But instead of worrying about how long you might be in it, instead focus on the fact that you are doing it – now – and that it will help you arrive at a better place in your life and happiness.

Psychodynamic therapy is quite an analytical process that aims to get at the feelings deep down that cause psychological problems. (Most often it is used with people who have had traumatic childhoods.) This sort of talking therapy is not so widely available on the NHS any more, although if a doctor offers you six counselling sessions, it could be that the counsellor you get is trained in psychodynamic therapy. But it's more likely you will be offered CBT instead, so if you really do want this kind of therapy, be aware that you may well have to go private and pay for it.

Relationship (and sex) therapy

Our relationships with our partners are so fundamental to our general happiness. As we all know, they don't always go according to plan and so, often, we don't feel brave enough to talk to our partners without someone there to help us. There are many therapists and organisations (like Relate – www.relate.org. uk) who are there to help if difficulties have gone too far or if the relationship has become abusive. These therapies can help get your relationships back on track, help you deal with the pain of an affair, or help you both to agree a calmer ending … it all depends on what you need it to do. These therapists don't take sides, they are there to listen to each of you, to teach you how to communicate with one another without resorting to shouting, insults or other nasty language. It teaches you how to listen, to give and take, and hopefully to start to find the best in one another again. Or at least to respect one another enough to part on good terms.

Sex therapy may be part of relationship therapy, or it can be used on its own to help you and your partner find what is fulfilling for you both, how to deal with tricky issues like past sexual abuse that might be making a loving sexual relationship difficult, or to deal with more tricky sexual problems. In this case, too, remember these are experts who have seen it ALL and who are trained to help you. And it is not about getting naked with your therapist – unlike in the movies! (But you will probably be given 'homework'…)

There is some relationship and sex therapy available on the NHS – though there is usually quite a waiting list and it is not available everywhere. But if you live in a large city, there is a chance your GP may be able to refer you to a psychosexual clinic.

Hypnosis

Hypnosis is another treatment that you may be offered. And it certainly helped me. It is not at all like those stage hypnotist acts you might have seen where people are put in a trance and then told to act like idiots! It is just a kind of relaxed state which – when you're in it – can help you access and influence parts of your mind that normally feel less accessible.

The hypnotic state is a natural one that many of us lapse into every day. When you walk from the bus into your office and suddenly realise that you don't actually remember crossing the road this morning, you have been in a type of hypnotic state or trance. In other words, your mind has been elsewhere while your body has been on autopilot. Some people find they can deliberately take themselves into this deeply relaxed state. Others learn it from tapes or books.

Hypnosis is sometimes used in the NHS to help people with psychological problems. It is often also used for conditions such as irritable bowel syndrome. There are also plenty of private practitioners around, and they can help with all sorts of goals, including weight loss, giving up smoking and confidence-building. Hypnosis can also be used as a great stress-buster.

If you decide to have hypnosis privately, do find a practitioner through a professional organization such as the National Council for Hypnotherapy (www.hypnotherapists.org.uk).

Getting the most out of your therapy

Through talking you will uncover your feelings and you might even discover some surprises along the way. A therapist once said to me that people's emotions are like an onion. They have lots and lots of tiny thin layers, which need peeling off one by one before you reach what's going on inside. After about five or six sessions you might start unpeeling the layers.

Not everyone can open up quickly, but the rewards can be worth it in the end if you battle your fear and just do it. Be committed to the work and visualise a time in the future when you'll be strong. Again, think of it like going to the gym – you're not going to have the body of Elle Macpherson after one day on the treadmill! But keep your goals in mind (and don't compare yourself now to what you think you should be).

It took me some time to open up to my therapist. For the first few sessions it seemed ridiculous and like nothing was happening. But as the trust built and my therapist helped me peel off some of the layers, it was incredible how much I discovered was going on inside me and by releasing all that pent-up emotion in a safe place with someone I trusted, it began to ease the burden I'd been carrying.

I heard from a woman named Lisa, 45, who went to see a therapist when she was struggling to come to terms with being diagnosed with cancer. Her therapy didn't just involve talking about the cancer itself; she also talked about how her husband had left her with three young kids five years earlier. She'd never talked about it, but realised this was making her cancer diagnosis especially hard for her to accept. She unravelled how she was actually not only worried about her health but was still hurting over the treatment her husband had dished out. She'd needed to talk about that more and finally, once she had, she could let go of her anger towards him. This in turn made it possible for her to spend all her energy focusing on her health.

Often, talking about feelings is upsetting, especially if they are locked deep inside you. This might even feel very negative and overwhelming, but this can be part of the process and, believe me, if you stick with it you can arrive at a positive conclusion, or reach a place where you can be more at peace with your mind and heart. Think of yourself as a pressure cooker – you have to let the steam out. Things will feel a bit hot and difficult for a while, and then you can breathe a sigh of relief again. Once the painful stuff has spilled out, you have a better chance of moving on completely. It's not going to happen overnight, but each step is a step closer to what you want.

Getting help: points to remember

o **Mind over matter.** Having a strong and healthy mind is just as important as having a healthy body. If you want to get the most out of life, good mental health is key.

o **Asking for help is a sign of strength.** It takes guts to admit to your failings and dedication to want to overcome them.

o **You're not the only one who needs help.** With one in four people in the UK suffering from mental health issues at some point in their life, you're certainly not alone. If you need further proof, ask yourself why there's a whole industry devoted to mental health and therapy?

o **Help comes in many forms** – whether it's talking to a friend, finding a support group or accepting professional help. And when it comes to therapy, there are different techniques and specialisms. Knowing what you want to achieve or fix makes it easier to find the right help.

o **There's a reason why they're called experts.** We can't always fix ourselves – often we (or our families) just don't have the skills required. Professionals do, and they are there to help.

o **Getting to the bottom of your problems is the most effective way to solve them.** But finding the root of an issue or worry can take time, patience and strength, and you can't always do it alone.

o **The journey may be difficult but the destination is worth it.** Talking to a therapist can be daunting, and dealing with your issues can be painful or hard work, but stick with it – you'll be rewarded with peace and happiness at the other end.

CHAPTER 15

Setbacks and plateaus

As irritating as they are, setbacks and plateaus in our progress are a normal part of reaching our goals, whether dating, trying to lose weight or working towards any kind of healing. They may be frustrating or painful, but setbacks and plateaus aren't failures by any stretch of the imagination. I sure had plenty of them in my recovery when things seemed to stall or even slide, like when certain operations didn't work and needed redoing, or when at the first trial there was a hung jury over whether Danny was guilty of rape. In these cases, we need to dig deep, keep our faith and just carry on fighting. If I hadn't, we wouldn't have got the conviction on the second trial and I'd probably have given up on any further recovery. In this chapter we'll talk about how to keep yourself focused on the end goal so that you can survive any setback.

It's a setback, not a failure!

When you are moving on well with your goals, sometimes a blip can throw you, or even seem to completely halt your progress. These need not be seen as failures, as long as you keep looking forward and work through them so that they don't kill your inspiration. Not losing sight of your end goal can be tricky when things aren't happening as fast you'd hoped or appear to be standing still altogether. The journey we're on is not always smooth, but thinking of these bumps as failures is just negative and makes us feel as if we've done something wrong, whereas seeing them as 'setbacks' gives you a chance to pause and take stock before carrying on. And sometimes our setbacks open up all kinds of opportunities for us that we didn't even notice before.

One of my worst setbacks was after I'd had six operations on my oesophagus. The doctors had some terribly grim news.

'We're afraid your oesophagus keeps closing up,' they warned.

'What can you do?' I asked.

I didn't like the serious look on their faces. I grabbed Mum's hand and we just listened. I'll never forget the feeling of horror when they told me what they thought the next step should be.

'We need to remove your small intestine and make an oesophagus out of that,' one doctor said. 'You may need a colostomy bag then.'

After everything, after all I had been through, I couldn't believe this setback. It seemed enormous, overwhelming and dreadfully unfair.

I put my hands over my face and sobbed. Usually Mum was the first to encourage me to see the positive side. But in this instance she broke down too. We cried together for a bit. It really was bad news and seemed so unfair. Luckily, we kept hopeful and waited it out and things did get better again. I didn't need that major operation in the end, but by then I had talked myself out of the initial shock and disappointment and resolved that what was far more important was that I had my life and that if I could deal with all the other crap that had been thrown at me, I could deal with this too.

Casey, 26, witnessed a similar feeling as she tried to help her sister Veronica overcome anorexia. Veronica would work hard to make progress, but then her emotions would take over and she would slip back into not eating. Every time Veronica had a relapse and lost more weight, Casey insisted it was just a setback and that Veronica shouldn't give up trying.

'If I'd told her: "Right, you've failed again!" then her confidence, which was already low, would have fallen further. So we just called these her setbacks and brushed them off, and then would get thinking about how we'd move on from there. That way Veronica always thought there was hope and never gave up trying even after she'd cried in complete despair at what she was going through. And she knew that we weren't giving up on her.'

This is such a loving response, and it really helped poor Veronica to know not only that she could move on from her setbacks, but that her family could too.

Even though I've come through the main part of my recovery and my life is mostly back on track, I still have the occasional setback. Four years on from the attack, in the midst of setting up my charity, I suddenly found myself having a panic attack in the car on the way to work one day. My mind had started to go over what had happened again – I could even smell the same smells as when the acid hit my face.

'Oh my goodness!' I thought in horror. 'The attack happened nearly four years ago! Maybe I am not over this after all?'

Tips to get through setbacks

You may feel like the world is fighting against all your hard work and trying to undermine it, but remember that everyone who has ever overcome adversity, no matter how big or small, has probably faced lots of challenges along the way. In order to recover from setbacks and not lose faith, I learned these lessons:

1) Accept the setback. Of course this is easier said than done, but just start by deciding to accept it and then let the feelings of acceptance follow. This will allow you to keep a clear head so you can get back on track. Instead of railing against it with 'why me?', have a cry, take stock and then think: 'Right, what next?' Then take whatever practical approach comes to mind or take advice from those closest to you.

2) Keep the goal clearly in sight. Even if the goal posts have shifted, that doesn't mean you have to throw everything away. You just have to try something different until you get moving again, even if it means you're moving in a new direction.

3) Learn from your setbacks. During my operations, I had so many setbacks that I lost count! I suffered many times from an annoying lingering infection when a skin graft wouldn't heal

The incident scared me and my thoughts all seemed to backslide. It even made me worry that perhaps I wasn't a suitable candidate to run a charity after all. 'How can you be advising other people to get help when you clearly need it yourself?' I thought. It felt like a major setback and I was quite worried, so I decided to go and get professional advice to see why this was happening. I went to see a hypnotherapist who helped me with more CBT properly. I had to try and take it on the chin (as it were!) and just keep focused on the end goal, which was to recover. I did what the doctors told me, such as taking my antibiotics on time or making sure my diet was good to help me recover. I just stuck to whatever advice I was given, and looked forward to recovering. Of course this was hard at times and felt never-ending, but I accepted it and never lost sight of my goal to get well.

4) Nothing is predictable. So you're on a journey onwards and upwards, right? But en route you might be thrown a curve ball that takes you by surprise. You might have a blip. This is all normal and can actually be helpful sometimes. You can be even better when you reach the goal! If you plan your life to never have surprises, then you won't ever be prepared to deal with them. And believe me, they will happen.

5) Be inspired by the past. Normally it's best not to dwell on what's been, but in the case of setbacks it can actually be helpful sometimes to go back and think of times when you got through a difficult time. Think of times when you were convinced you would fail...but you didn't. This will help you remember how you coped and will motivate you to get past your current setback.

work. It really helped guide me through my feelings and learn to control them again.

'Is it normal for me to feel like this even though I am stronger?' I asked her.

'Absolutely,' she reassured. 'It's just your brain's way of processing what's happened again and reminding you that you might still need a little help every now and then to keep recovering.' This, to me, was so reassuring. It meant I was able to see the setback for what it was – just a blip – and carry on moving forward.

Eva, 22, wrote to me when she didn't get a place on the uni course she wanted, despite studying incredibly hard:

> '*I only took my A levels to go to university and study fashion design. I couldn't believe it when the competition was so tough I couldn't get in. Now I might as well give up.*'

Thankfully though, with help, Eva thought of other ways into the fashion industry and found a business course, which it turned out was far more suited to her talents. What could have been dismissed as a huge failure became just a setback, but really it sent her on a happier and more productive path altogether and she's even started her own online business selling her friends' fashion designs. This is such a great example of taking a step back and saying to yourself, 'Well, if that didn't work, what will?' instead of just being defeated when things don't quite go as we hoped. But it's not always straightforward to work out what's happening when a setback strikes.

The never-ending plateau – time to hold tighter to your goals

Plateaus are when after making so much upward and forward progress, things seem to stop moving on any further. Like setbacks, these can also be tough times and annoyingly trying on our patience. If you've ever tried to lose weight or get fit, you will really know what I mean. It's easy to lose loads of weight in the first couple of months, but then it seems to slow down or even stop. It can be so demoralising when you've been trying very hard.

I had my own plateau after my first documentary was aired. I was so excited and happy about people's reactions and feeling so positive. Then everyone sort of forgot about it and I was still at home with my parents, still with no job, still facing operations. It was a case of 'now what?' I felt like I was stuck in limbo. I found myself feeling impatient for the next big change in my life. But actually it was a time that taught me to calm down and take stock again of the good things that were around me. I also took time to digest what had happened before I planned my next move. It was then I decided that I was ready to move out, to be independent and start working again.

As much as whizzing through life making the most of it is good, there is also nothing wrong with just 'coasting' for a bit and feeling a sense of contentment about where you are and how much you've moved on, before you start thinking about what you want next. You can't make giant leaps and bounds every single day. How exhausting would that be anyway?

But some plateaus can be infuriating. I've heard of athletes who train so hard, push themselves so far and yet still hit a wall where they just can't seem to reach their ultimate goal. Sometimes, however hard you try and do something, not much happens – for a while anyway. It's during these moments that the people who will ultimately succeed in their goals choose to do something different to those who will eventually give up; they ride with it and allow themselves to enjoy the journey, and they start to think creatively about how to get unstuck. They take it as a given that there will be plateaus, that nothing can be exciting all the time and that we need the lull in order to enjoy the success.

Of course there is nothing to stop you from breaking up a plateau a little if boredom and complacency have truly set in. You can use it as motivation, as long as you are doing something positive and not just thrill-seeking or looking for instant happiness. If you're stuck in a rut, it is possible to do something today to get out of it, even if it has nothing to do with your immediate goals. Try something completely different – even little things can help. If you always shop in the same place, switch supermarkets, just to get a change of scenery. If you always wear black, wear red – I bet it'll start a conversation with the people you work with! If you want to be more specific about your goals, like if you keep meeting the wrong men on internet dates – try joining a social group or take a course to widen the net. Sometimes a mentor or friend is the best person to give an 'outsider's' point of view, to give ideas about how to help you out of your rut. Ruts often look like quite dark places but mentors and friends can see over the top and give you a bunk up if necessary!

It is possible to make mundane plateaus more pleasant too. When I was having on-going surgery on my eye I had to go to an eye clinic four times a week and to say it was boring is an understatement! But every time my Mum and I went, we stopped for a coffee and a biscuit, we had a chat and tried to make it as pleasant as possible. Every week I tried to see it as a 'milestone' as my eye improved and blindness was avoided (but the biscuit and chat was probably what we were really looking forward to!). In the end it felt like a big achievement and though at the time it felt boring and pointless, we tried to inject something nice into the experience.

Ultimately, though, the whole of life cannot be one exciting thing after another. You have to experience the 'quiet' moments and take time to reflect, in order to appreciate the exciting stuff. In my opinion, the most boring people in the world are those who complain of 'being bored'– there is always something to enjoy, even in the boring times.

> **'Focus on the journey, not the destination. Joy is found not in finishing an activity but in doing it.'**
> Greg Anderson, founder of the US Wellness Project

Putting up with pain in order to get greater gain

I learned the hard way that putting up with indignity and pain was what was needed if I was going to make the best recovery possible. I later discovered that psychologists say being able to live with discomfort in this way, and also being able to put a hold on our happiness or comfort for the meantime, is essential to good mental health. It made me feel great to find out that what I was doing meant I was really sane and grounded!

We often have to put up with discomfort in order to succeed later on. Like when you are revising for an exam – it's tempting to go out with your mates, but you know that if you stay in and study, you've got a much better chance of passing that exam, and your job prospects will probably improve. And sometimes we have to go without that cream cake that we want right now, in order to have a slimmer body on our holidays!

There are lots of examples. But just remember: next time you feel that what you want is on hold so that you can one day have something better, you are just proving what a mentally healthy person you are.

Playing the 'long game': there are no quick fixes

Quick fixes always seem tempting. Sure, they might make us feel good right now, but they're often the easy way out. The relief they can bring is wonderful sometimes, but very rarely do they work long term. I think a healthy and realistic way forward is accepting that most things in life worth having mean putting up a bit of a fight, working hard and enduring peaks and troughs. It's easy to feel that when things go wrong we are right back at the beginning of our struggle. But this is never true. Ask yourself what is different now from how it was at the beginning of your journey. And list all the advances you have made and lessons learned since you began.

Also, if you view the bigger picture rather than focusing on short-term fixes you're less likely to see plateaus as negative and feel like you are stuck. You can see them as momentary setbacks full of opportunity to learn and grow. As I said before, psychologists have told me that good mental health is all about being able to delay having something nice in order to have something even better later on.

Learning to be flexible in your strategy is a big part of this. When I was a child, I never drew pictures of myself being disfigured. I drew a pretty girl with a husband, a boy and a girl child, a dog, a cat and a house with roses around the front door; all the clichés! But I still think anything is possible for me, I am just going about it a different way and there is nothing wrong with that. And maybe I'll never have kids or I'll adopt or be happy without them. I just know the girl in the drawing is going to find peace and contentment whatever she is doing, even if the picture is different to the one drawn by my five-year-old self!

Setbacks and plateaus: points to remember

o **Setbacks aren't failures!** They're an inevitable part of working towards a long-term goal, so don't let them kill your motivation - keep your end goal in sight and you'll be moving forward again before you know it.

o **The road may be bumpy, but it still leads somewhere.** See the bigger picture of your recovery, take note of your ups and downs, and learn to be flexible when obstacles appear so that you can get round them on the way to your destination.

o **You can learn valuable lessons from your setbacks.** If something's happened once, you'll be much better informed to stop it happening again. You may even discover some valuable shortcuts to help you catch up or get ahead in your recovery.

o **It's important to pause and take stock.** Make the most of setbacks or plateaus as the perfect opportunity to stop and re-assess your situation.

o **No pain, no gain.** The best things in life are worth fighting for, so be strong enough to put up with anything - including difficult setbacks or boring plateaus - confident in the knowledge that your reward will come later.

CHAPTER 16

Getting stronger – and staying stronger

It's time to celebrate: you're gaining control of your life! As you start to get stronger, so many aspects of your life seem to change. You'll be amazed at how you start to see the world around you. At the same time, the people in your life will start to see you in new ways too. Most will celebrate with you, which is amazing. Some may have a harder time getting used to the stronger you. In this chapter we'll look at how to embrace and get used to your positive new life, how to stay compassionate when others aren't ready for you to be independent and strong, and how not to let anyone try to drag you back down. We'll also look at staying in touch with the things that keep you feeling strong.

You've made it!

As you chip away at your negative thinking, listen to your positive voice and start to take healthy risks - no matter how hard it seems - one day it *will* happen: you *will* feel stronger. Gradually, bit by bit, life will feel easier, you'll feel more capable, and then you'll have made it through your toughest times. Congratulations! You will always have areas you want to develop and you will certainly always have goals and dreams to continue working towards, but your hard work has paid off. You've started to take control of your life. *You* did it!

My own journey has been very long, with so many tiny goals and steps that I achieved along the way. I can't pinpoint the exact moment when I knew I'd 'made it', but that doesn't matter. It happened. And gradually it will happen for you too.

Even once you are stronger, the journey hasn't ended – not completely. In many ways we have more adjusting to do with our new 'strong' selves and we may face new and different challenges. These challenges remain personal to us – it's for no one else to judge them. I may be strong enough to stand up and talk about my charity at a public event or walk down a red carpet and be interviewed on camera, but if I had to walk up to a stranger on the street and ask for directions to the Tube, I'd probably still feel very self-conscious! It may sound silly, but it's one of the things I'm still working through and so I don't beat myself up about it. Equally, while I know I am able to cope with life's big difficulties and all the repercussions, something as small and material as my BlackBerry breaking can make me really cross and upset! I am just human. We all are.

We still need to be kind to ourselves, even when we're stronger. The journey of life and its challenges never ends completely, so be careful not to fall into the trap of thinking: 'Right, that's it, everything's sorted now,' else you'll set yourself up for disappointment. There will be blips in life, but that's okay. The good news is that you can use your newfound strengths for the next set of challenges, which will make them easier to deal with.

You *know* you can get through things now. How comforting is that?

At first, after any period of emotional suffering, we might find ourselves left only with our own thoughts when the worst of the experience is over. After my stay in hospital, I went from having lots of people around me all the time, to silence at home in my bedroom – and that was when I had to find my real strength.

I had a letter from a woman named Sally that I could really relate to. Her boyfriend Darren died in a car accident and she was left alone to look after their two young kids. 'At first everyone was around, calling, dropping off flowers, offering to help with the kids, taking time off work. Then, after a month and once the funeral had passed, people stopped being in contact as much and went back to their own lives. That was when I knew I had to be strong for the kids. The grief was overwhelming and it took a whole year to deal with the worst of it. By then I did feel stronger, but it was hard to adjust. I'd never felt more alone and I had to find other strengths.'

Having achieved your aim of making it through, you can find yourself getting to know the new *you* and discovering a new identity. Sally told me how she'd always been 'Darren's girl' and lived her life through the kids. Later on she'd got involved in a group that helped other single mums and even became the chair-person for their meetings, something she'd never have dared do before. As her newfound skills developed she found herself having to set boundaries so that she wasn't taken advantage of, and at the same time she also found other forms of happiness through her new social group and the confidence she had developed.

Reaching your goal doesn't necessarily mean you'll feel comfortable straight away though, so be kind to yourself while you get used to it. We have to learn gradually to feel comfortable with where we are now. Even if something is really good for us, when it's new it can feel unnatural. But this will pass. Dawn French found this when she recently lost eight stone in weight. She said she had been so used to her old body and knew how it worked, and she just wasn't yet used to her new, thinner one! I also had to learn who I was again from scratch, but because I'd faced such a big challenge I'd already proved to myself I could manage. I had loads of strength and resilience now to face the challenges in my new life! There's was something so very liberating about that.

How others may react to the new you

Some of the people who helped you when you were at your weakest may have taken great pride in doing so. They may have felt needed and valuable because they were able to give you support, for which I'm sure you were incredibly grateful. But once you are stronger, sometimes the reactions from these same people or others can be surprising. Most people will likely help you celebrate all your wins and be thrilled to see your newfound confidence, but do be prepared that others may find it harder to get used to the new, stronger you. They may have challenging things going on inside their heads that make it hard for them to adapt, perhaps making them criticise you for moving on at a speed they think is inappropriate. Or they might feel purposeless once you get stronger. They might worry that you don't need them any more, and that they're no longer valued, no matter how much you try to reassure them. They may even seem angry at you for changing, or feel like you've abandoned them after being 'in it together'.

Although you can and should be grateful and compassionate for all they did, if someone is struggling to accept your new strength this is not your problem to fix. That may sound hard, and I don't mean that you shouldn't be kind, but your strength may have brought up issues in them that only they can address, and you simply don't need to indulge people who make you feel guilty for getting on with your life. On the other hand, do remember to say thanks to people who have helped you, and be careful not to abandon those who were with you throughout the hard and difficult times. (And if you've received negative reactions, might this be the cause?) Maybe it's time to use your strength to help them get stronger.

It might also be that some people just felt more comfortable with you when you were suffering or weak. They don't know how to act around you now you are stronger, or they may even drop out of your life altogether. This is sad, but again you just have to accept that this is their problem and not yours. Or your strength might spark jealousy within someone. I've had comments on Twitter where people have accused me of looking too glam or trying too hard to conform! But actually I'm just being me and making the best of myself. I know I don't have to answer to these people and I think compassionately that they may just have trouble being happy for others. I don't take it personally, even if I don't like what is being said. I also try not to engage in a negative conversation about it – that does nobody any good.

Sometimes people even feel unnerved by people who are brave enough to show their strength. Even though Heather Mills isn't always popular, she is an example of someone who gets a lot of stick, not only for her behaviour sometimes, but I think often for her strength too. People seem to think it's okay to laugh and make jokes about the fact she is an amputee, perhaps because she is so strong in every other way. It's a bit like this for Madonna too. She never shows weakness or moans in interviews about feeling fat or hating her body, or how heartbroken she is after her relationship breakdowns. She just gets on with it, and yet the amount of criticism levelled at her is huge! People envy strength in lots of ways.

When you are strong, people can develop unreasonably high expectations of you – sometimes they think you can get through anything! Through my charity work I met an amazing lady called Vera. She is a great campaigner, a bit of a feminist and a lovely, warm person who is always smiling, is never down, and who gives so much. When her husband died suddenly, she was inundated with cards. 'You're so strong, we know you'll get through it,' many people wrote. Although the sentiment was lovely, people just didn't acknowledge that she was actually terribly sad and broken inside. While grieving, what she really wanted was for someone to step in and comfort her and understand her pain.

Similarly, people have said to me: 'But it's been easy for you. And you've been on TV.' But the reality is that no matter how easy it looks now, or the fact that I've smiled throughout all my pain, I worked incredibly hard to get here and at times it was horrible. I've started everything from scratch, including putting my own money into setting up the charity. It's never easy for anyone to recover from trauma or upset, even if you're in the public eye.

As I grew stronger, I found that people everywhere wanted to share their problems with me, which is an amazing honour. But it has happened at inappropriate times too! I forgive this and understand it – I think because I am strong now, people feel comfortable telling me so much! For example, when I first began dating again, I realised I attracted men who only wanted to talk about their problems and nothing else! I'd get dressed up, looking forward to a night of fun and getting to know someone new, but they would start reeling off reasons why they were unhappy or what terrible childhoods they'd had. Maybe they thought that if they had problems too, I'd like them more. Of course, I'd love to help them all, but it just wasn't the right time or place. It was sad that they only saw me as a person to lean on, not a potential girlfriend! I had to learn to deal with this, too.

Staying compassionate

Once we've found our own strength it's important not to judge other people who may not have found theirs. It's easy to look at other people's situations and think: 'Oh goodness, it's so much easier for you, so just stop moaning and look at what I've had to go through!' But remember, in the same way it was for you, if someone has an issue in their lives that *feels* like a problem, then it *is* a problem and it's not for you to judge.

I had a friend, Tanya, who did this. She'd suffered from so much bad luck and had been through the mill, with a series of family bereavements and losing her job. But the way she'd dealt with it all was really admirable! She would still come out for a meal or come dancing in a bar with a smile on her face. But then a mutual friend of ours started worrying about her weight and became obsessed with her stomach, constantly asking us to look at it from different angles and complaining how bloated she felt. She would avoid meeting us for drinks because her worries over her stomach (which was tiny really!) seemed to overtake everything. Of course, in comparison to Tanya's bereavements and job problems, this weight obsession appeared tiny, and Tanya struggled to remain compassionate. 'For God's sake,' she snapped one day. 'That girl needs to experience serious problems to know what a problem really is!'

But to our mutual friend her weight was a serious problem and I felt sorry for her. It had taken over her life, whether or not it made sense. She'd not had to deal with anything else serious in her life that could help put things in perspective. And maybe her image problems masked an underlying issue in her life that she wasn't telling us about.

So instead of criticising friends for their problems, try to support them. Chat to them and find out what's really going on. Also know when to take a step back – remember that you cannot help everyone and not everyone wants to be helped, but find other ways to support them and always be ready to offer your help if they ask for it, as a compassionate friend should.

Go back to what gave you strength in the first place!

When you're in a better emotional place, it's tempting to think you can discard the tools that helped get you there. After all, you don't need them any more, right? But actually, you might find you need a top up at some point, so it's wise to keep these tools handy, just in case.

My relationship with my parents changed enormously after my attack. I felt so much closer to them than I ever thought possible, I appreciated them and all they did for me so much more. I loved having them there during my recovery and now I want to help them in any small way I can. Even when things are going well, I want to share it with them. I like to visit them as often as I can. Even though I don't need them with me all the time for me to cope with my life, the strength I got from them during my recovery is something that is reinforced every time I see them. I feel the same about my therapy – it's something I know I can always return to if necessary, and sometimes do when I'm suffering setbacks or moments of doubt.

If you are able to recognise which things helped you in the past, you should use these tools again if it makes sense. I now know that therapy can be incredibly useful because I've already benefited from it, just as I know spending time with my family helps make me feel better. And just because you ask for help or confide in someone about how you're feeling, it does not mean you are weak or have slid backwards. You have just learned to recognise that what helped you last time will help you again.

Maria, 24, wrote to me about something similar after her dad had died:

'To begin with I was a complete mess. He'd been ill for so long, but nothing prepared me for his passing. We were especially close as we were a single parent family. During this time, a friend I wasn't especially close to had also suffered a bereavement and in a strange way it pulled us closer together as we could confide in each other, even though grief is a very personal thing. Now on anniversaries, Christmasses and birthdays, we always make time for each other, share our feelings, and are very kind to each other and it really helps. Even though we're both feeling stronger these days, we still get more strength from it.'

You'll probably also find new ways to keep strong. I enjoy boxing, believe it or not, which is great for dealing with anger – we all need an outlet for our frustrations or anxieties that inevitably crop up in day-to-day life! But it is also a good form of exercise and helps me burn off excess emotion during any ups and downs. Exercise is something I know makes me feel good, so I've made it a regular part of my routine now. Anything creative like painting, reading or writing, or musical hobbies can be helpful in keeping you strong during wobbly moments, and they provide a healthy break from hard emotions. Doing the things you love will help you to remain strong and in touch with yourself. It seems simple, but too often we forget to keep going

My top five things that help me stay strong

1) Ringing my mum every day to talk through the events of the day or to get extra support. I still have bad days, like everyone else, and sometimes I just need to have a good cry down the phone to her! But she shares the good times too and I love talking to her.

2) Exercise and healthy eating. This helps keep me strong in body and that definitely helps my mind. I find that boxing is such a great outlet to take out any frustrations and gives me a buzz.

3) Writing things down. I still do it even though I am in a happier place. I jot down the good and bad times and inspiring things, and if I am feeling stuck I read back what I've written to see how much life has moved on.

with the things that give us pleasure, and we let other things start to get in the way.

Strength comes from so many areas in our lives. It comes from our mind – in the form of positive thinking and looking for the best in a situation. It comes from our belief system – knowing that we're doing the right thing for ourselves and having the faith that things will work out. We also get strength from sources outside of ourselves, such as therapy, family or love. Once we have found this strength, the key to remaining strong is in not being afraid to top it up – to give our inner strength a boost by turning to the tools and resources that helped us become strong in the first place.

4) Re-reading the books, poems and quotes that have helped inspire me. I love doing this. There is nothing like curling up with a book you know makes you feel stronger and re-reading the best bits. (See my list of favourite books on pages 283–4!)

5) Returning to therapy when I need it. I am not afraid to ask for help. I am not afraid to get a professional's point of view. Instead of trying to diagnose myself, I just reach out and let someone else who is trained do it.

Why not make a list of five things that you know will always help *you*?

Getting stronger and staying strong: points to remember

o **Recovery is not the end of the road.** Your goals have been reached, so it's time to set new ones! With your newfound strength and skills, the journey to achieve your dreams will now be easier than ever!

o **It can take time to get used to the new you.** Your new strength and confidence might feel unnatural at first, so take it slowly and keep being kind to yourself as they settle in.

o **Remember to say thanks to those who helped.** If they shared your lows, let them share your highs, too. It's only fair.

o **Your recovery is *your* recovery.** Most people will want to celebrate it with you. But if others don't, who cares?! Quickly check you haven't forgotten to thank them, then get on with your new life and don't let anyone bring you down.

o **Be prepared that other people may start to lean on you.** You're now a great example of strength and recovery, so don't be surprised if people look to you for help and advice. Share it if you're ready, but remember to set boundaries and don't feel you have to give too much of yourself if you're not comfortable doing so!

o **Be compassionate.** Your recovery has been a success, but other people may still be working through their own issues. They must go through all the same stages as you did – in their own time and their own way. So don't judge them or compare their journey with your own. Just give them support.

o **Keep your tools handy for when you need a top-up.** Identify what things helped make you stronger and be willing to turn to them when you need a boost. Also keep your eyes open for great new ways to maintain your strength and self-esteem.

Final thoughts

Although I've been lucky enough to have the opportunity to write this book, at the end of the day I'm just a normal girl who survived something terrible and I hope that by sharing my story, and how I coped, I have helped you too.

Four years ago I was wishing myself dead in a hospital bed, unable to bear the sight of what was left of my face. I couldn't envisage a life beyond that morning when I awoke, let alone having a proper future. Dealing with severe health problems and all the physical pain that goes with it was hard, but dealing with the psychological impact of fear and, later on, discrimination from other people, felt far, far too much for me to bear. I really had to dig deep and explore parts of my soul I never had before to even attempt to overcome it. But, in time, I found out that I was resilient, determined and strong, and that my sense of humour had survived – despite everything!

People have called me special, but I don't think there's anything particularly special about what I've done. I didn't do anything brave, I didn't choose for this to happen to me. I've just recovered in the only way I knew how, and had good and bad days like everyone else. And you know what? I still do!

Once I sobbed to mum: 'Why has this happened to me? Why have I been given this life?' And she replied: 'Because you're strong enough to live it!' But I didn't believe her at the time. Like everyone else, I've had triumphs and failures. I've fallen down many, many times on this journey, but I've always tried to get back up as quickly as possible and not look back to where I fell. More than anything, I've tried not to dwell on my time in the bad places ... and there have been a few! It's when we get up after the fall – that's what makes us strong.

Without a doubt I'm hugely grateful to my family, my doctor and everyone else who supported me – they've been my rocks – but what I've learned is that the only person who can pull you out of the pit of despair is *you*. I know this is possible, because I've done it myself.

Today, as I sit and write this, my difficult journey is still far from over. I'll have many more operations to my face to manage my scarring. There's a chance of health problems from having general anesthetic over 100 times in the past few years. People still stare and point at me on the street (except that sometimes now they can't quite work out what's wrong or if I've had Botox!) And I know I'll face more discrimination and perhaps, even, that my dreams won't all be fulfilled. But I also know now that *whatever* happens next I will cope and will keep going. Having been through so much is strangely liberating, because I know now that whatever life throws at me I can deal with it. And I plan to enjoy every minute of it! I hope you will come to see life in this way, too.

Please believe me when I say that even in your darkest hour there is a way out. There is always light, even if you can't quite see it to begin with. I can promise you: *things do get better*. I am living proof of that!

Katie

My daughter Katie's story has touched the lives of so many because it's such an extraordinary one, and as her mother I'm so very proud.

Four years ago, I didn't envisage a future for her at all. When we arrived at the hospital after a stranger threw acid in her face, she was an unrecognisable, bloodied mess. Her father had to sign a form to give permission for surgeons to remove her cheek, nose, chin and eyelids; half of her face.

This situation was so awful for us it was surreal. My beautiful daughter, whose ambition was to be a model and TV presenter lay before us in a broken state that no parent should ever have to see. It was expected she'd be half blind, left unable to swallow or do anything for herself again. There didn't seem to be any way back from this.

I gave up my job and accepted I'd be her carer for life. We were told to take things day by day and just hope for the best. But then, even in her hospital bed and barely able to see, there were glimmers of hope. As Katie lay with black, white and brown patches of skin from corpses draped over her, in order to preserve her face, she asked us how she looked.

'You have different patches all over you,' I said nervously. But somehow she managed to laugh.

'I'm like a patchwork doll!' she said, trying to smile.

Although Katie's body was broken, we soon discovered that her spirit wasn't. Very quickly we let her take the lead in being cheerful. It was impossible for my husband and me to be disheartened when she was so obviously prepared to fight.

And what a battle it has been. Katie has been to the brink of despair at times, facing so many terribly painful operations, not to mention the ordeal of getting her attackers jailed. There have been down days when she has just sobbed. But those were rare. With a courage I never knew she possessed, she has tackled each and every challenge with faith and hope, providing inspiration to those around her too. She has certainly inspired me and her brother Paul and sister Suzy. All along we have thought: 'If she can do this, so can we.'

When Katie first mentioned doing a documentary I wasn't sure if it was something we should be involved with. It seemed very strange to allow cameras into our private family home to show Katie at such a vulnerable time. As a mother I just wanted to protect her from people's stares and judgments. But the reality was that it helped enormously in the end. Not only did it increase people's awareness of disfigurement but it gave Katie a sense of acceptance from the outside world; something that has been pivotal to her recovery. Afterwards, when Katie told us she wanted to start a charity to help other people, we felt protective of her once again and feared she might struggle. She wasn't very good with computers or especially organised. But with her classic sense of positivity and determination, she said: 'I will try and find a way and if I can't I'll ask someone to help me.'

Just two years after her attack we were standing waiting to hear Katie speak at the opening of her charity, The Katie Piper

Foundation. Although she was shaking with nerves beforehand, we watched her effortlessly give a speech in front of a hundred people, including Simon Cowell. And her dad and I could barely see through our tears of pride and joy.

How far Katie has come in such a short period of time is nothing short of a miracle. It doesn't surprise me that she's become an inspirational figure to others, and her willingness now to help other people on their journeys through many types of pain is just wonderful. None of this has been easy for Katie, but with her gritty determination and good sense of humour, and even with the odds stacked completely against her, she has won the fight so far. I could not be more proud of her.

Diane Piper

Resources

When we're feeling low or struggling through bad times, there are many places we can look to for comfort, encouragement or inspiration. In this section I've listed some of the books, music and films and real-life survival stories that helped me find strength during my recovery, which you may find helpful, comforting or motivating too. Reading or watching something poignant or inspirational can often remind you that you're not alone in your suffering. On pages 286–96, I've also included contact details for organisations you can turn to in times of trouble. There are many more out there which you can find on the internet, but these are some reputable organisations to get you started.

Music: soul food

Music has the power to evoke an amazing range of different feelings – some songs can make us feel inspired or uplifted, while others may sooth or calm us. During difficult times, it can be a great relief from your pain to lose yourself in music, and to find meaning or significance in song lyrics. During my recovery, a friend kindly put together a CD of elevating songs to help me get through those dark early days. Many of them had powerful messages of how to be a survivor. I loved that CD and have included some of the tracks on the list below, along with my other favourite 'fear buster' songs. And I'm sure you'll have plenty more favourites to add to your own playlist.

- 'Man In the Mirror' by Michael Jackson
- 'You Are Not Alone' by Michael Jackson
- 'Beat It' by Michael Jackson
- 'Chariots of Fire' by Vangelis
- 'Believer' by Christine Milian (I used to listen to this before auditions)
- 'Hero' by Mariah Carey
- 'Make It Through the Rain' by Mariah Carey
- 'Can't Take That Away' by Mariah Carey
- 'For Once In My Life' by Stevie Wonder
- 'Rise and Fall' by Craig David featuring Sting
- 'Something Inside So Strong' by Labi Siffre
- 'Dear Friend' by Stacie Orrico
- 'Survivor' by Destiny's Child
- 'Beautiful' by Christina Aguilera

Books to boost you

Great stories and books of advice have always helped people through difficult times. Some doctors even 'prescribe' patients spiritually enhancing books to read. While I was recovering at home and couldn't face going outside, I did a lot of reading. My favourite books include real-life accounts of people who have triumphed over tragic events in their lives. Even if you haven't suffered the same situation, their experiences and the positive ways in which they survive help you consider your own approach to life and show how much courage human beings are capable of! I also loved books of affirmations which just gave me a little reminder every day to stay strong and keep my heart open. There are also many self-help books which can give you the tools and skills to cope with the things that life throws at you. Here I've listed some of the books I found personally inspiring, and also some books on specific topics by experts, which I recommend and which may be of particular help to you.

- *A Random Act*, by Cindi Broaddus
- *Tiny Dancer*, by Anthony Flacco
- *The Other Hand*, by Chris Cleve
- *The Other Side of Nowhere*, by Daniella Westbrook
- *Anyone Can Do It*, by Duncan Bannatyne
- *Walking Tall*, by Simon Weston
- *It's Not About the Bike*, by Lance Armstrong
- *The Diary of Anne Frank*
- *The Five People You Meet In Heaven*, by Mitch Albom
- *The Secret*, by Rhonda Byrne (see pages 92–3 for more information)
- *The Rules of Life* and *The Rules of Love*, by Richard Templar
- *The Road Less Travelled*, by M. Scott Peck
- *Feeling Good: The New Mood Therapy*, by David D. Burns
- *Man's Search for Meaning*, by Viktor Frankl
- *Mind Over Mood*, by Greenberger and Padesky
- *How To Stop Worrying and Start Living*, by Dale Carnegie
- *Self-Esteem: Simple Steps to Develop Self-Worth and Heal Emotional Wounds*, by Gael Lindenfield
- *Overcoming Low Self-Esteem*, by Melanie Fennell

- *Overcoming Social Anxiety and Shyness*, by Gillian Butler
- *Overcoming Depression*, by Paul Gilbert
- *Overcoming Childhood Trauma*, by Helen Kennerley
- *Developing Resilience*, by Michael Neenan
- *Authentic Happiness*, by Martin Seligman
- *Breaking Free – Help for Survivors of Child Sexual Abuse*, by Ainscough and Toon
- *Loving Yourself Loving Another: The Importance of Self-Esteem for Successful Relationships*, by Julia Cole

Favourite films

Have you ever sat in front of a film and felt transported into another world, and then when it finished felt as if you've woken from a dream? Great films can really allow us into the minds and lives of other people and teach us so much about many different issues and situations. Here is a list of some powerful films that I found gave me a big boost and something to take away and think about afterwards.

- *The Blind Side*, starring Sandra Bullock
- *Philadelphia*, starring Tom Hanks
- *Million Dollar Baby*, starring Hilary Swank
- *My Left Foot*, starring Daniel Day-Lewis
- *Dangerous Minds*, starring Michelle Pfeiffer
- *Dead Poets Society*, starring Robin Williams
- *Good Will Hunting*, starring Matt Damon
- *Forrest Gump*, starring Tom Hanks
- *Erin Brockovich*, starring Julia Roberts
- *A Beautiful Mind*, starring Russell Crowe
- *The Diving Bell and the Butterfly*

Organisations and Charities

These are some of the main UK support organisations which you or someone you know can turn to in times of need, or even if you just want a bit of extra support. All of these have excellent websites, where you can find useful information and resources and many also have helplines offering immediate counselling or advice. Whatever you are going through, there is a specialist charity or organisation out there that can help. If you don't see what you're looking for here, there are many more charities that you can find online. Please don't hesitate to get in touch with these organisations – they are waiting and ready to help you.

Immediate help:

Samaritans
08457 90 90 90
www.samaritans.org
For immediate support when you've reached rock bottom or feel you want to harm yourself, always ring the Samaritans. As I've mentioned previously, there is a kind person available for you to talk to 24/7 and they can help you to deal with all kinds of problems, or else direct you to someone who can.

Childline
0800 1111
www.childline.org.uk
Childline is a counselling helpline specifically for children and young people. If you're under 18 and don't know where to turn, Childline's trained counsellors can help you get things off your chest and talk through your options. Calls are completely confidential and will never appear on your phone bill.

Depression, anxiety or fear:

Rethink

0300 5000 927

www.rethink.org

Offering support and advice for people living with mental illness, Rethink provides an advice helpline, downloadable factsheets and access to support groups. They also campaign to challenge attitudes towards mental illness.

Mind

0300 123 3393

www.mind.org.uk

Mind's aim is to make sure anyone with a mental health problem has somewhere to turn for support so they can live a full life and play their part in society. Mind provides information and advice, training programmes, and grants and services through a network of local associations. They also provide training and consultancy for employers on the topic of mental health in the workplace.

Depression Alliance

0845 123 23 20 *(this isn't a helpline, but you can call to request an information pack)*

www.depressionalliance.org

The leading UK charity for people suffering from depression. They provide information and support services to those who are affected, via publications, support services and a network of self-help groups.

Anxiety UK

08444 775 774

www.anxietyuk.org.uk

A charity providing support for anxiety conditions, including phobias. Their range of services includes a national UK helpline, staffed by people who have themselves lived with anxiety, as well as therapy services in a range of locations and even a webcam and telephone therapy service for those in areas where there are no available therapists, or who struggle to get out of the house.

No Panic

0800 138 8889

www.nopanic.org.uk

A voluntary charity who offers support for sufferers of panic attacks, phobias, obsessive compulsive disorders and other related anxiety disorders. As well as the helpline, they provide telephone recovery groups, literature, books, CDs & DVDs to help overcome anxiety disorders, and step-by-step written recovery programmes for phobias and OCD (obsessive–compulsive disorder).

OCD Action (Obsessive Compulsive Disorder)

0845 390 6232

www.ocdaction.org.uk

Support and information for anybody affected by obsessive-compulsive disorder, a type of anxiety condition where people suffer from obsessive thinking or fears they cannot control, or behaviour and rituals such as cleaning their hands many times a day, checking things are safe over and over, counting things, repeating words or phrases, etc. They offer a helpline and email support, regional support groups and online resources including information on treatment. They also work to raise awareness of the disorder amongst the public and frontline healthcare workers.

There is more information about OCD, including fact sheets, on the **Royal College of Psychiatrists** website: www.rcpsych.ac.uk/ mentalhealthinfoforall/problems/obsessivecompulsivedisorder. aspx

Under 25s:

Get Connected
0808 808 4994
www.getconnected.org.uk
A free and confidential helpline for young people who know they need help but don't know where to find it. Help also available by email and webchat.

Youth Access
www.youthaccess.org.uk/directory/
A directory of free counselling services for young people across the UK on a wide range of topics.

Young Minds
0808 802 5544 *(helpline for parents)*
www.youngminds.org.uk
Committed to improving the emotional well-being and mental health of children and young people. Also provides expert knowledge to professionals, parents and young people through our helpline and online resources, training and development, outreach work and publications.

Self-esteem and happiness:

Be Mindful

www.bemindful.co.uk

Mindfulness is a technique recommended by psychologists for helping people to deal with trauma. It can help you change the way you think about experiences and reduce stress and anxiety (see pages 19–20 and 243 for more information). This site from the Mental Health Foundation has in-depth information about the Mindfulness approach.

Action for Happiness

www.actionforhappiness.org

A movement for positive social change, bringing together people from all walks of life to play a part in creating a happier society for everyone.

Also try searching for the topic of self-esteem on the NetDoctor website (see page 294). You'll find a wealth of information and advice, as well as a clever test that can help you recognise and boost your confidence levels.

Eating disorders:

Beat

0845 634 1414

www.b-eat.co.uk

This is the national UK support organisation for eating disorders, offering help to those suffering from Anorexia, Bulimia or Binge Eating Disorder, as well as providing support for their family and friends.

Addictions or advice about drugs:

Alcoholics Anonymous
0845 769 7555

www.alcoholics-anonymous.org.uk

This well-known organisation helps alcoholics to recover and gain control of their addiction via a 12-step programme and a network of groups and meetings where people can share their experience, strength and hope with others.

Gamblers Anonymous
www.gamblersanonymous.org.uk

A fellowship of people who have joined together to do something about their problem with gambling and to help others do the same. Includes a forum and information about regional meetings.

Frank
0800 77 66 00

www.talktofrank.com

Comprehensive information about drugs, including where to get help and a confidential advice helpline.

Bereavement:

Cruse Bereavement Care
0844 477 9400

www.crusebereavement.org.uk

A national charity offering free, confidential help through their telephone helpline, online information and face-to-face support in branches from trained volunteers to bereaved people coping with grief.

RD4U

0808 808 1677

www.rd4u.org.uk

This is Cruse's youth service, offering help to young people in coping with the death of someone close to them.

Relationships and sexual issues:

Relate

0300 100 1234

www.relate.org.uk

Relate is a national charity that offers advice and counselling on relationship problems, including difficulties within a relationship, separation and divorce, sexual concerns and issues such as heartbreak or rejection. Relate operates throughout England, Wales and Northern Ireland. (In Scotland, Relationships Scotland offers a similar service.) Relate is not usually free but is generally more affordable than the private sector, and rates take into account the means of the client. Relate counsellors have very thorough training and help countless individuals and couples every year.

Refuge

0808 2000 247

www.refuge.org.uk

Offers advice on dealing with domestic violence. They offer a support helpline and a network of safe houses that can provide emergency accommodation for women or children at risk.

FPA

0845 122 8690

www.fpa.org.uk

A sexual health charity offering straightforward information, advice and support on sexual health, sex and relationships to everyone in the UK.

Brook
0808 802 1234
www.brook.org.uk
Free and confidential advice for under 25s on sexual concerns, contraception, STIs and family planning.

Finding a therapist:

NHS Therapy
www.nhs.uk/Livewell/counselling/Pages/Accesstotherapy.aspx
Information from the NHS about finding therapy, with details about both free and private services.

British Association for Counselling and Psychotherapy
www.itsgoodtotalk.org.uk/therapists/
This directory lets you search for and find a private therapist based on your needs, location and criteria.

UK Council for Psychotherapy
http://members.psychotherapy.org.uk/find-a-therapist/
Search for psychotherapists and psychotherapeutic counsellors who are accredited practitioners on the UKCP register.

Counselling Directory
www.counselling-directory.org.uk
A search-directory listing counsellors and psychotherapists who are registered with a recognised professional body or with professional qualifications.

British Association for Behavioural and Cognitive Psychotherapies (BABCP)

www.babcp.com

An organisation specifically for CBT therapists, the website includes a searchable online register of accredited practitioners as well as a wealth of information about CBT.

Medical advice:

NHS Direct

www.nhsdirect.nhs.uk

If you're worried about your health, this is your first port of call for checking your symptoms so that you can put your mind at ease or know where to look for further help.

NetDoctor

www.netdoctor.co.uk

The UK's leading independent health website is a collaboration between committed doctors, health care professionals, information specialists and patients. NetDoctor provides a wealth of infor-mation about both physical and mental conditions, symptoms, treatments and healthy living, as well as forums and an online consultation service.

Burns, scars or disfigurement:

The Katie Piper Foundation

www.katiepiperfoundation.org.uk

This is the charity I worked so hard to set up – our aim is to progress and improve the rehabilitation and scar management available to burns survivors, and to provide information on and access to non-surgical treatments for burns and scars. It has also become a support network for people living with burns and disfigurement, both through workshops and events and through the online forum: *www.katiepiperfoundation.org.uk/the-kpf-forum*.

Changing Faces
0300 012 0275
www.changingfaces.org.uk
A national UK charity that supports and represents people with disfigurements, marks or scars affecting the face or body. They offer advice and information on skin camouflage, as well as advice on handling social situations and how to develop self-esteem and gain self-confidence.

Children's Burns Trust
www.cbtrust.org.uk
A national fundraising charity dedicated to providing rehabilitation support for burned and scald-injured children and their families. They campaign for awareness and prevention and fund research into pioneering surgical and psychological healing techniques.

Career or life choices:

Learn Direct
0800 101 901
www.learndirect.co.uk
An e-learning organisation that lets you gain new skills and nationally recognised qualifications.

Open University
0845 300 60 90
www.open.ac.uk
High-quality distance learning to enable people to achieve their career and life goals studying at times and in places to suit them.

Volunteering:

Do It

www.do-it.org.uk

An organisation and search facility committed to making sure that those who want to volunteer can do so quickly and easily.

Volunteering England

www.volunteering.org.uk

An independent charity supporting, enabling and celebrating volunteering in all its diversity. Has a network of accredited Volunteer Centres dedicated to helping people find volunteering opportunities in their local area.

Volunteer Scotland

www.volunteerscotland.org.uk

Volunteering Wales

www.volunteering-wales.net

For volunteering in **Northern Ireland**, visit www.nidirect.gov.uk/ find-voluntary-work-in-the-uk

Acknowledgements

To my amazing parents, you always told me things get better – and you were right. Thank you for never letting me give up – or lie in bed!! Dad, you showed me how to laugh in the face of evil and smile through the pain. You really were right, laughter is the best medicine. Thank you for keeping the whole family positive and alive! Thank you to my beautiful mother who told me that giving up is not an option. Mum, your patience, dignity and determination helped me through the impossible.

Thank you to my two best friends; my darling brother and sister Paul and Suzy ('Biff and Dinky'). All those notes, poems and good luck charms you gave to me made feel I was never alone and that I had you by my side both physically and mentally. Thank you for showing me that with friendship, support and love you can make it. Paul, you show us all with your crazy running that it really is mind over matter and that you can achieve anything you set out to do. Suzy, my full-time counsellor, you're always there to listen, help and understand whatever time of day or night. You're the best 'twin' a sister could want.

Thank you to my tireless team at The Katie Piper Foundation – I am so lucky to work with such an incredible bunch of women … and a few men! Your passion, enthusiasm and dedication motivates me daily. Thank you for making it easier for all of us survivors to live with burns and scars.

I would also like to say a huge thank you to all my Twitter followers and everybody who has written to me or approached me in the street to give their continued support. Knowing everybody is behind me has helped me so much and has been instrumental in the writing of this book – so thank you. You are all amazing!

A big thank you to Jenny Heller and Ione Walder and all the teams at Quercus involved in the making of this book, including Shannon Kyle, psychotherapist Christine Webber, Helena Caldon and the great cover team: Ray Burmiston, Tara Mears, Claire Wacey and Jenny Richards. It was such an amazing experience from the first time we sat around the table with an exciting vision to finally holding this book in our hands. Thank you for making my dream a reality and for all your hard work and efforts in getting it just right!

The publishers would also like to thank Ted Baker, 18 and East, Topshop and Zara for supplying clothes for the cover photography.